Susan Weingarten

Haroset
A Taste of Jewish History

The Toby Press

Haroset: A Taste of Jewish History

The Toby Press LLC
POB 8531, New Milford, CT 06776–8531, USA
& POB 2455, London W1A 5WY, England
www.tobypress.com

ISBN 978-1-59264-516-9, *hardcover*

A CIP catalogue record for this title is available from the British Library

Printed and bound in the United States

In memory of my mother, who would have approved of this one

Contents

Acknowledgments

The idea for this book came from a seminar given by Vered Noam at Tel Aviv University, where I was a guest. Vered asked me whether there were any Greek or Roman foods that resembled haroset, and my search started from there. It has taken longer than I expected. Many of my friends and family have listened to me for some time now talking about haroset, with endless patience and enlightening comments.

Micky read and commented on almost all of it, and Andrew Dalby and Ranon Katzoff have read earlier drafts – to them my especial thanks. Some of the material was presented at the Oxford Symposium on Food and Cookery in 2005 and 2011, where many symposiasts listened and made helpful and encouraging comments, and even followed up with references. In particular, I am grateful to Val Mars who gave me a recipe and instructed me about liripipes, to Sammi Zubaida who taught me how to pronounce *hallek*, to Andrew Dalby and Sally Grainger for their discussions in detail of *oxyporium* and Apicius.

I am also grateful to Rabbi Yekutiel Cohen for clarifying references in his book, and providing me with more, and similarly to Rabbi Yaakov Weingarten for his book and his reminder about wheelbarrows; to my son Amos who laid the resources of the library in the Yeshivat

Hesder at Kiryat Shemona at my disposal and patiently instructed his mother about *Rishonim* and *Aharonim* alike; to Nicholas de Lange who discussed *embamma*; to Simha Goldin who directed me to Israel Yuval's enlightening ideas on haroset in the Middle Ages; to Aharon Werbner who sat up all night looking for haroset in the works of Rabbi Nahman of Breslov; to John Cooper for his time and his book; to Guy Stroumsa for discussion of blood libels; to David Curwin of the blog Balashon who introduced me to Zanolini. For many years now, I have been fortunate enough to have had the help and support of Aharon Oppenheimer and Yuval Shahar in all my research; here too they have been invaluable. Youval Rotman and Sylvie Honigman have sat and listened over coffee, and even invited me to present aspects of haroset at their seminars.

I am grateful for the financial support of the Jane Grigson Trust and the GIF: the German-Israeli Foundation for Scientific Research and Development. My German colleagues from our GIF project on Food in the Ancient World, Werner Eck and Georg Schäfer from the University of Cologne, have contributed many helpful discussions.

I am indebted to the head of Koren Publishing, Matthew Miller, and the editor-in-chief of Maggid Books, Gila Fine, for taking on my book and believing in it, and for putting it in the hands of their dedicated editors, Ita Olesker and Shira Koppel. In particular, I am grateful to Nechama Unterman, so much more than a "mere" copyeditor/proofreader, who has saved me from some of my own mistakes. I did not expect such true professionalism.

And last but not least, I am grateful to all the women and men who freely gave me their recipes and told me how they make their haroset today.

Susan Weingarten
Jerusalem, Rosh HaShana 5779 – September 2018

Introduction: Texts and Tastes

> But when from a long-distant past nothing subsists, after the people are dead, after the things are broken and scattered, still, alone, more fragile, but with more vitality, more unsubstantial, more persistent, more faithful, the smell and taste of things remain poised a long time, like souls, ready to remind us, waiting and hoping for their moment, amid the ruins of all the rest: and bear unfaltering, in the tiny and almost impalpable drop of their essence, the vast structure of recollection.
>
> Marcel Proust, *Remembrance of Things Past*[1]

For around two thousand years, Jews have celebrated the Passover Seder in their homes every spring, using texts and tastes to join themselves to their history. The Seder commemorates the Exodus of the Children of Israel from slavery in Egypt to freedom. It is a dramatic ritual that includes reading the text of the Passover Haggada, pointing out and eating symbolic foods and drinking four symbolic cups of wine.

Unlike the other symbolic Passover foods, haroset has always been something of a mystery. It was not one of the three original symbolic foods eaten at the first Passover in Egypt. It first appears in the

---

1. Marcel Proust, *Remembrance of Things Past: Swann's Way* (=À la recherche du temps perdu: du côté de chez Swann), trans. C. K. Scott-Moncrieff (New York: Random House, 1934), 36.

Mishna, but with no explanation of why, and with few details of what it was made of or what it tasted like. The Talmuds tell us that haroset was said to resemble the mud or clay for the bricks made by the Children of Israel as slaves in Egypt, so it was clearly connected to the story of the redemption from an early stage, but we do not know when it arrived at the Seder.[2] It seems to have been introduced to counteract the bitter herbs, which have been part of the Passover meal since the time of the Exodus.

Throughout the generations, in fact, the rabbis have given different and sometimes contradictory explanations of haroset. This book is my attempt to solve the riddle of the origins of haroset – when and why it appeared, what it was made of and how it changed over the generations.

PASSOVER FOODS AND JEWISH IDENTITY

Eating and experiencing food involves all our senses, especially smell and taste. Thus the power of eating to conjure up memory is great. Perhaps the most famous modern literary example is an episode in Marcel Proust's *Remembrance of Things Past*. There the narrator takes a *petite madeleine*, a little cake, dips it in his tea and eats it, and the taste and smell conjure up overwhelming memories of his childhood.

I do not know whether Proust, an assimilated Jew, ever took part in a Passover Seder. But long before he wrote, eating symbolic foods on Passover was deliberately used to summon up memories. Long before the Haggada was written, the biblical Book of Exodus tells us exactly what foods were to be eaten at the first Passover meal, the meal eaten in haste before the Jews left Egypt (Ex. 12:1–11). First and foremost was the paschal lamb, to be eaten together with matza, the unleavened bread that is called the "bread of affliction," and *maror*, bitter herbs. These clearly relate to the bitterness of the life the Israelites led in Egypt, as described earlier in Exodus (1:13–14):

---

2. The Hebrew word I have translated here as clay or mud, *teet*, is usually translated into English as "mortar," which is used to stick bricks together, rather than the mud or clay used to make the bricks, which is clearly what the rabbis meant.

And Egypt made the children of Israel to serve with rigour. And they made their lives bitter with hard bondage, in mortar, and in brick, and in all manner of bondage in the field.[3]

Detailed instructions are also given for how to prepare the food (Ex. 12:1–11), and then the text adds:

And this day shall be unto you for a memorial; and you shall keep it as a feast to the Lord; throughout your generations shall you keep it as a feast by an ordinance forever. (Ex. 12:14)

The biblical Passover feast is thus intended to create a historical memory in the future. The Israelites leaving slavery for freedom are to establish their new identity with the foods of the Passover meal.[4]

"Tell me what you eat and I will tell you who you are," said the nineteenth-century French philosopher Brillat-Savarin. Thus in the Book of Exodus, every family of the People of Israel is instructed to take the "abomination of Egypt," later specified as a lamb. Jews are to show themselves as *not* Egyptian: they are to sacrifice the lamb, sprinkle its blood on the threshold of their houses, roast it and eat it. Eating the meat of the lamb signified their freedom from the Egyptians. The text makes it clear how important this is in creating a Jewish identity. In the future, each Jewish family is instructed to take their lamb to the place ordained by God (later identified with the Temple in Jerusalem), offer it as a sacrifice and eat it with bitter herbs and matza:

Thou shalt therefore sacrifice the passover [offering] unto the Lord thy God … in the place which the Lord shall choose to place

---

3. This translation has been taken from the adaptation of the Authorized Version by Harold Fisch in *The Jerusalem Bible* (Jerusalem: Koren, 1989). Fisch uses Hebrew transliterations for proper names, but I have preferred the English versions which are still perhaps more familiar to an English-speaking audience.

4. See on this: Georg Schäfer and Susan Weingarten, "Celebrating Purim and Passover: Food and Memory in the Creation of Jewish Identity," in *Celebration: Proceedings of the Oxford Symposium on Food and Cookery 2011*, ed. M. McWilliams (Totnes: Prospect Books, 2012), 316–25.

His name there. Thou shalt eat no leavened bread with it; seven days shalt thou eat unleavened bread with it, the bread of affliction … *that thou mayest remember* the day when thou camest out of the land of Egypt all the days of thy life. (Deut. 16:1f., my italics)

After the destruction of the Temple, Jews stopped sacrificing lambs, but continued to eat matza and bitter herbs, each family in its own home. Thus the celebration of Passover, with its distinctive foods prescribed by the Bible, became an integral part of being Jewish.

The biblical text telescopes past, present and future. The words are addressed to Israel in an uncertain future, "in the place which the Lord shall choose," about the past deliverance which is to be remembered all the days of their lives. The specific foods of Passover are being used here to create memory – prospectively. As the antiquated "thou" of the translation tells us, the instruction, while addressed to the whole Jewish people, is given in the singular. Every Jew is to see her- or himself as if s/he was personally redeemed from Egypt. Each individual thus becomes a representative of the communal whole, whose personal memories represent the memory of the whole people.

I am not aware of any other ancient textual evidence of using food in this sort of symbolic way before the rise of Christianity. Judaism is unusual in this regard. But over time various cultures have used food as a means of underlining memories. Recently, the anthropologist David Sutton has explored the relationship between food and memory on a modern Greek island in his book *Remembrance of Repasts*.[5] He discusses the use of ritual acts of eating in creating memory, and in particular prospective memory. He distinguishes between "inscribed memory," written records, and "incorporated memory," which results from a "performance" involving eating. Many of Sutton's Greek islanders are now scattered throughout their own diaspora, and the memories conjured up by food serve to remind them of an entire cultural world they have lost. This is an experience very similar to the much longer Jewish experience of loss and diaspora.

---

5. David E. Sutton, *Remembrance of Repasts: An Anthropology of Food and Memory* (Berg: Oxford/New York, 2001).

These concepts of food and memory will aid us in looking at haroset: the biblical and rabbinic injunctions as part of the process of creating prospective memory; the part played by both inscribed and incorporated memories; and the construction of a Jewish cultural world in the Diaspora. Haroset has been eaten by Jews as part of the rituals of Passover for generations, throughout many countries in the Diaspora. And the rabbis who write about haroset in the Talmud from the very first describe it too as a memory or memorial, *zekher*. As we look at its development, we shall return to these concepts of food and memory to examine how it is related to individual and community memories.

THE HISTORY OF HAROSET

It is only recently that historians have become aware of how much the history of food and its preparation can contribute to the study of general history. What people ate and how they prepared it was, and still is, an important part of how people lived. In this book, I shall be tracing the history of haroset and exploring how its development over time contributed a chapter to Jewish history – a longer and more complex chapter than we might have thought.

After the destruction of the Second Temple in the year 70 CE, a gap opened at the heart of Judaism. Until then, Jews had centered their worship of God on His Temple in Jerusalem. Now this was no more. The rabbis thus set about re-creating Judaism. Temple rituals were moved to synagogue and home, including the rituals of Passover. Judaism was re-centered on the study of texts constructed by the rabbis for posterity in the talmudic literature, the Mishna, Tosefta, Talmuds and Midrashim.[6] These texts recorded rabbinical debates and exegesis; they were written and rewritten, collated and edited over the centuries after the destruction of the Temple, in the Land of Israel and in the Babylonian Diaspora. Ever since that time, all rabbinic discussions refer back to the talmudic literature as their foundational reference point. The written text, surrounded by commentaries, replaced the Temple as the focal point of Judaism. This new center was portable and it accompanied the Jews throughout their dispersion.

---

6. You will find an explanation of what the Mishna, Tosefta, Talmuds and other sources are in the next chapter.

This situation held good until what may be seen as the second revolution in Judaism, the Enlightenment. This movement proposed substituting rational and scientific thought for tradition and faith. Until then, Jewish writing had been almost entirely the preserve of the rabbis. From then on we are witness to new kinds of Jewish literature – secular, rationalist, historicizing, belletristic. Rabbinical literature, however, does not cease, and while the main stream of textual study and commentary continues, we also find other channels of expression – mystical, messianic but also rationalist.

The history of haroset and its development reflect these patterns of Jewish history. I shall trace the development of haroset from its unclear origins in the Land of Israel to its presence today wherever in the world there is a Jewish community. Haroset probably already existed toward the end of the time of the Second Temple, when the Land of Israel was under Roman domination. Some customs of the Seder, like the requirement to "recline" while eating, have parallels in Greek and Roman banquets. Can we perhaps find anything like haroset in a Roman cookery book?

I shall begin my narrative looking in detail at the talmudic sources, which form the basis for later rabbinical discussions of haroset. Until modern times, after all, it has been mainly the rabbis who were concerned with recording and recommending what went into haroset.

The rabbis of the Mishna, who are the first to mention haroset by name, tell us almost nothing about it. It was clearly by that time (the beginning of the third century CE) a part of the Passover Seder, but we are left in the dark as to how it arrived or what it represented, and there is only the slightest hint of what it was made of. By talmudic times (roughly the fourth to the seventh centuries CE), however, rabbis in both the Land of Israel and in Babylonia were recorded discussing with one another how to make it, and what it symbolized.

This interest continued through the ages, with many rabbis suggesting recipes for haroset and the proper way to make it. Often they disagreed, and sometimes they changed their minds, and ordinary people clearly did not always follow the rabbis' recommendations.

By looking at haroset in this way, we shall see how its ingredients changed, and with them its taste; today it is almost invariably sweet, but at other times it was sweet-and-sour, bitter, or even just sour. Sour tastes were very popular in Europe in the Middle Ages, for example, and I shall try and relate the changes in haroset to the wider historical and geographical context.

As the Jews moved through the different countries of the Diaspora, different ingredients became more or less available, and the rabbis were often forced to endorse new ingredients in retrospect. By the Middle Ages, the generations of rabbis called the Tosafists were recommending the inclusion of fruits mentioned in the Song of Songs that symbolized the Jewish people. The story of haroset became intimately linked to this beautiful biblical book. I will look closely at the fruits, nuts and spices of the Song of Songs, and what they symbolized.

European Christians of the Middle Ages – the so-called Dark Ages – were often antagonistic to Jews and highly suspicious of their customs. Eastertide reminded them of the crucifixion of Jesus, and their anger was often directed at local Jewish communities. In particular, the long incomprehensible Hebrew rituals and the strange and unidentifiable foods of the Seder held around this time of the year seem to have become extremely suspect in their eyes. We shall see how haroset, often diluted with red wine or vinegar, became connected to the terrible accusations of the blood libels.

Much of the information about haroset can be gained from medieval and modern commentaries on the Talmud, or explanations of the text of the Passover Haggada. Apart from these commentaries, there is other literature about haroset: medieval and modern poetry, novels and short stories. The romantic German Jewish poet Heinrich Heine is justly famous for his description of *cholent*, the heavy Sabbath stew, but he also wrote about haroset, as did the American Jewish dramatist David Mamet.

In the Middle Ages, a new tradition of illustrating Haggadas began, which continues to this day, and the pictures and their captions tell us yet more about how haroset was made and distributed. These enhance the educational effectiveness of the Seder – parents telling the story to their children. Over the ages, almost every educational device possible has been used to keep the children's interest high through the long night, but word plays and games with language also form a serious part of the story of haroset.

The twentieth and twenty-first centuries have brought about many changes in foodways all over the world. Today there seems to be a never-ending search for novelty, for new tastes. How has this movement affected haroset? And what about the counter-movement, the search for "authenticity"?

When writing about food in the twenty-first century, we cannot avoid the gender aspects. While preparing food in the home has been almost entirely the province of women throughout history, haroset was, and still is, often made by men. Why?

Finally, I have interviewed a number of women and men from different Jewish communities for this book. Each of them told me about his or her family origins, and how they (or their husbands or wives) make their version of haroset. The younger women often sent me to their mothers or mothers-in-law for more information. I conclude with their very different recipes, and my gratitude.

Chapter 1

On the Origins of Haroset

We are in Jerusalem in the springtime. The air is clear, the countryside still green after the winter rains. The Temple glints gold and white from the top of Mount Moriah. The streets are crowded with tired and thirsty pilgrims, bleating sheep, excited children. And among the sounds of the city we hear the spice merchants crying their wares: "Come buy your spices for the mitzva."

Even if my picture above of Passover in ancient Jerusalem owes something to my imagination, the cries of the spice merchants appear in both the Jerusalem and Babylonian Talmuds. R. Elazar b. Tzadok, who lived in Jerusalem when the Temple still stood, quoted these words of the spice sellers as proof that haroset was considered to be a mitzva, a religious requirement, and not just a custom.[1] This is the first hint we have of haroset – a vivid phrase that conjures up the smell and taste of the Jewish past.

---

1.   Pesaḥim 116a; Y. Pesaḥim 37d.

THE CREATION OF THE SEDER

As we noted in the introduction, following the destruction of the Second Temple in the year 70 CE, Jews were no longer able to celebrate Passover by going on pilgrimage to Jerusalem and eating the traditional foods in the Temple courts. A vacuum was left at the heart of Judaism. The rabbis, concerned with the survival of the Jewish people, worked to reinstitute Judaism in new forms. Thus the ancient Passover Temple rituals were reconstructed as the Seder meal which took place in every Jewish home, following the text of the Haggada. "Haggada" means narrative, and by narrating to his family the story of the slavery and redemption of the Jews in Egypt, the head of every Jewish household was now actively and personally involved in ensuring the survival of the religion and its traditions.

Since the Seder ritual was new and important, the rabbis were concerned with getting it right; from the very first time the legal codes were written down we find long and detailed discussions of it among the laws of Passover. These Passover laws get a whole tractate to themselves, Pesaḥim, in the Mishna, the early code of Jewish law, and in the subsequent Jerusalem and Babylonian Talmuds. Although the extent of the rabbis' influence over their Jewish contemporaries at this time is disputed,[2] their directions for the Passover Seder took deep root among Jews and are followed to this day.

While the Temple still stood, Jews would come on pilgrimage to Jerusalem to celebrate Passover, sacrificing the paschal lamb in the courts of the Temple and eating it there in Jerusalem with matza and bitter herbs. Many Jews would even come from abroad to Jerusalem, although clearly not everyone could come from far away. So how did they celebrate Passover? And what happened in the Land of Israel after the destruction of the Temple, but before the rabbis instituted the Seder at home? When was the Haggada written? It is difficult to answer these questions. But it is clear that the Passover Haggada as we have it today must have changed and developed over time, for it differs in places from

---

2. Seth Schwartz, *Imperialism and Jewish Society 200 BCE–640 CE: Jews, Christians and Muslims from the Ancient to the Modern World* (Princeton: Princeton University Press, 2001).

the instructions about Passover in the Mishna and the Tosefta.[3] Several fragments of early Haggadas from around the tenth century have survived in the Cairo Genizah, and these too show different customs from our present day Haggada. Thus there is a gap in our knowledge of the celebration of Passover from Temple times to the Haggada as we have it today.

The beginnings of haroset fall somewhere in this gap. Scholars differ as to whether it is possible to reconstruct any of the lost early narrative from the later sources. Can we read back any of the practices of the Haggada into earlier periods? I shall try to do this here, with due caution, noting difficulties as I come across them.

Haroset was undoubtedly a food of ordinary people, and it might even have been an everyday food at one time. It is possible that haroset was the Hebrew name of a Greco-Roman food in common use, called *embamma*. The Seder after all, in its reinvention by the rabbis after the destruction of the Temple, seems to have been built, at least in part, on the model of a Greco-Roman *symposium* meal. Thus I will be using contemporaneous Greco-Roman sources as part of my attempted reconstruction. But haroset differs from most other everyday foods in that it was singled out and used as one of the symbolic foods on the Passover Seder table. I shall now go back to look at what our earliest sources have to say about it.

What Are Talmudic Sources?

Since the earliest information about haroset is found in the talmudic sources, and many later rabbis refer back to them, a brief explanation of what they are seems in place here for the uninitiated. Apart from the laws written in the Bible, Jewish tradition has additional laws. These were originally preserved orally, but eventually written down in a collection called the Mishna, which was finally edited at the beginning of the third century CE by Rabbi Judah HaNasi – Rabbi Judah the Prince or Patriarch – the leader of the Jewish community at the time. The Mishna received its final form in the Land of Israel, the Roman province

---

3. For explanations of the Mishna and Tosefta, see below: "What Are Talmudic Sources?"

of *Palaestina*, at the same time the Greek writer Athenaeus of Naucratis was writing his book on the Greco-Roman *symposium, The Deipnoso-phists* (The Philosophers at Dinner), in Egypt or, perhaps, in Rome itself.

The laws found in the Mishna cover many aspects of everyday life. However, they are written very concisely. So further explanation was needed, and a body of legal and moral discussion and commentary on the Mishna grew up. Eventually, this too was written down by rabbis in both the Land of Israel and in Babylonia around the fifth and seventh centuries respectively, to become the Talmud Yerushalmi and the Talmud Bavli, the Jerusalem (or Palestinian) and Babylonian Talmuds. These quote the Mishna sentence by sentence, together with the talmudic commentary on it, the Gemara. In the Land of Israel, there were other legal compilations called *baraitot* (singular *baraita*) such as the Tosefta. There are also further rabbinic commentaries from these times, often on books of the Bible, called Midrashim. Since not everyone could understand the Hebrew, the talmudic literature often used the local Jewish language, Aramaic, with a sprinkling of Greek words.

The rabbis of the Mishna and the Tosefta are called *Tanna'im*, while the rabbis of the Talmud are *Amora'im*. The later *Geonim* commented on the Talmud in Babylonia.

Rabbis did not always agree with each other, and their debates form the main body of the text. Many of their discussions are related to food. Talmudic literature was written in the same world as Greco-Roman or Persian literature, but it differs in one important respect. The non-Jewish literature was written by aristocrats for aristocrats – no one else could read or write – who were not interested in how food was prepared. This was the province of women and slaves. These upper-class men were interested only in finished products, and in luxury products in particular. Talmudic rabbis, on the other hand, were interested in every aspect of daily life in order to bring it under religious control. Often very poor themselves, they provided a good source of information about the everyday food of ordinary people.

Haroset in the Mishna

As we have noted, Passover is mentioned in the Bible, together with the eating of lamb, unleavened bread (matza) and bitter herbs (*maror*), but not haroset (Ex. 12:8). The first written evidence of haroset under its own name is found in Mishna Pesaḥim, which deals with rabbinic regulations about Passover. However, haroset is merely mentioned here, with no further details about its function, symbolism, ingredients or taste:

> They bring before [the leader of the Seder] unleavened bread (matza) and lettuce and the haroset, even though haroset is not a religious obligation (mitzva).
>
> R. Elazar b. Tzadok says: 'It *is* a religious obligation.'"
> (Mishna Pesaḥim 10:3)

A similar passage about haroset appears in the Tosefta (Pesaḥim 10:9). R. Elazar appears to have been a merchant who lived in Jerusalem before the destruction of the Temple (Tosefta Beitza 3:8). There are traditions about him in later literature, but it is not always easy to determine how far these are original traditions and how far they have been edited by later authors. Thus the Babylonian Talmud quotes R. Elazar as saying that merchants would cry the spices for haroset in the streets of Jerusalem, calling: "Come buy your spices for the mitzva [of haroset]" (Pesaḥim 116a).[4] The earlier Jerusalem Talmud had cited *tagarei Yerushalayim*, the merchants of Jerusalem, crying their spices (Y. Pesaḥim 37d). These texts suggest that Jews must have been eating haroset in Jerusalem together with their roast lamb and unleavened bread and bitter herbs *before* the Temple was destroyed. However, Tosefta Pisḥa writes of R. Elazar and the merchants of Lod (Lydda), a city in Judea, rather than Jerusalem. Perhaps, then, he was talking about the time *after* the destruction of the Temple (Tosefta Pisḥa 10:10).[5] In that case, the Mishna's discussion

---

4. I have translated this as "buy," though the literal meaning of the text is "take." However there are those who would disagree. Rabbi David, the grandson of Maimonides, for example, writes that the merchants were offering spices free. Dr. Don Krisst has suggested to me that this may have been ironic on the part of Rabbi David, given the high prices of spices at the time.
5. Here R. Elazar is quoted as saying to some merchants of Lod, "Come, buy your spices for the mitzva [of haroset]": S. Friedman, *Tosefta Atikta* (Ramat Gan: Bar Ilan University Press, 2002), 421–38. Friedman thinks that in this case the Tosefta ante-dates the Mishna, and the commoner "Jerusalem" was substituted for "Lod."

about whether or not haroset is a mitzva may indicate that this was a new element, which belonged to the rabbis' re-creation of the Passover rituals as the Seder held in every Jewish home, rather than something that stretched back to Passover in the Temple. Either way, R. Elazar certainly saw spices as an essential ingredient of haroset.

The Mishna continues, in words similar to those quoted today at every Passover Seder by the youngest child present: "On all other nights we dip our food once, on this night we dip twice" (Mishna Pesaḥim 10:4). The Mishna refers here to the everyday practice throughout the Roman Empire, among Jews and non-Jews alike, of dipping bread into a condiment at a meal (among the poorest this was sometimes the entire meal). But at the Seder, it says, we dip twice. Today, at the Seder, we first dip herbs into salt water, and then later, bitter herbs into haroset. In earlier times, herbs may have been ritually dipped into haroset twice at the Seder.[6] This custom seems to have persisted in some places until the early Middle Ages, when the *Or Zarua* disapproved of eating haroset before the second dipping with the bitter herbs.[7]

The bitter herbs themselves are specified in the Mishna: "And these are the herbs by [eating] which at Passover a man fulfills the mitzva: *ḥazeret, olshin, tamkha, harḥavina* and *maror*" (Mishna Pesaḥim 2:6). The Jerusalem Talmud clarifies two of these terms, explaining that *ḥazeret* is *ḥasa*, i.e. lettuce, while *olshin* is translated by the Greek words *entubin*, endives, or *troximon*, which refers to the raw vegetable salad that accompanied a meal. Lettuce was clearly bitter in those days, like wild lettuce is today. Neither the Mishna, nor the Tosefta, nor the Jerusalem Talmud explicitly says that the bitter herbs should be dipped

---

He proposes that Tosefta Pisḥa refers to a time *after* the destruction, when the rabbis assembled in Lod, rather than Jerusalem, as recorded in Tosefta Pisḥa 3:11. However, Friedman does not discuss the evidence of Tosefta Beitza that R. Elazar was "a merchant in Jerusalem all the days of his life."

6. Friedman (above, n. 5), *loc. cit.* Probably the ordinary herbs were first dipped into haroset too, instead of salt water, as today: J. Tabory, *JPS Commentary on the Haggadah: Historical Introduction, Translation and Commentary* (Philadelphia: Jewish Publication Society, 2008), 23–4.

7. He compared this practice with sleeping with one's betrothed before the wedding. Rabbi Isaac ben Moses, *Or Zarua*, ed. A. Marienberg (Jerusalem: Yeshivat Or Etzion, 2006).

into haroset, but this practice can be inferred from the Jerusalem Talmud and the later, more explicit discussion in the Babylonian Talmud (Y. Pesaḥim 37c–d; Pesaḥim 115a).

There is no discussion, however, in the Mishna of what haroset is. People were obviously expected to know. It is clear that haroset, though given special symbolic status at the Passover Seder, was in fact eaten all the year round, not just at Passover. We find instructions in Mishna Pesaḥim (2:8) that flour should not be added to haroset (or to mustard) on Passover in case they fermented and became *hametz*, leaven. The Babylonian Talmud mentions a special vessel for preparing haroset, called the *beit ḥaroset*, although it is unclear whether this existed in Palestine as well (Pesaḥim 30b). In the time of the Mishna, Jews were allowed to use most everyday crockery on Passover if it had been used for cold food only and then been cleaned. Use of the *beit ḥaroset*, however (as well as the *beit se'or*, the pot where sour dough was fermented for leavened bread), was forbidden "because it (the acidic haroset) also ferments very strongly" (Pesaḥim 114b), and both these pots were too difficult to clean properly.[8] Thus this everyday version of haroset apparently contained flour, which fermented and produced *hametz*, forbidden, of course, on Passover.

An Earlier Hint of Haroset?

Paradoxically, it is not the Mishna, a Jewish text, which has the earliest possible allusion to haroset, but a Christian one. The New Testament predated the third-century Mishna, and the famous "Last Supper" eaten by Jesus and his disciples before the crucifixion was most probably the Passover meal. Indeed, to this day, there are Christians who, wishing to re-create Jesus' experience, eat a form of Seder meal at Eastertide.

The Gospel of Matthew is considered by scholars to be the closest of all the Gospels to Jewish roots. It was probably written toward the end of the first century. It writes:

> And the disciples did as Jesus had appointed them; and they made ready the passover.

---

8. Perhaps they were made of wood.

> Now when the even was come, he sat down with the
> twelve [disciples]; and as they did eat he said, "Verily I say unto
> you, that one of you shall betray me."
>
> And they were exceeding sorrowful, and began every one
> of them to say unto him, "Lord, is it I?"
>
> And he answered and said, "He that dippeth his hand
> with me in the dish, the same will betray me." (Matt. 26:19–23)

Three verses later, the Gospel notes that Jesus "took bread and blessed it
and brake it," so the dipping in a dish mentioned in the text is unlikely
to refer to the common ancient practice of dipping bread into a condiment. It seems to be a separate dipping. Could the writer of the Gospel
possibly be referring to dipping bitter herbs into haroset?

As noted, it is not clear from the Mishna whether haroset was
used for dipping before the destruction of the Temple, or whether this
practice began when the rabbis re-created the Passover Seder. If Jesus
and his disciples did, in fact, dip bitter herbs into haroset, this would
bring us back to the time when the Temple still stood. However, here
too the evidence is unclear. The Gospel of Matthew was written some
time after the destruction of the Temple; we cannot know whether the
author is using a genuine tradition of what really happened at the Last
Supper, or whether he is describing the ritual of the Seder meal he knew
from his own times. If the tradition was authentic, Matthew's account
would be our earliest allusion to dipping bitter herbs in haroset.

There is further Christian evidence about bitter herbs at the Last
Supper, this time from the Church Father Jerome, writing in Bethlehem
in the fourth century, around the time of the Jerusalem Talmud. Jerome
had Jewish teachers and often shows that he knew their customs well.
He translated much of the Bible from Hebrew, and the New Testament
from Greek into the Latin Vulgate. In his Latin translation of the Gospel of Matthew, Jerome, surprisingly, translated the New Testament's
Greek word for the "dish" Jesus and Judas dipped into, *tryblion*, with
another Greek word, *paropsis*. The latter term usually refers to a little
side dish that held appetizers and sauce, *embamma*.[9] The word *paropsis*

---

9. Athenaeus, *Deipnosophists* ix, 368a, quoting Xenophon, *Cyropaedeia* i.3.4.

is also used for the food itself, and was used in particular to refer to bitter foods like edible bulbs – *bolboi* – and stalks.[10] Jerome's deliberate translation implies the use of bitter herbs and sauces. Is this because he had a tradition from the time of the New Testament, or was he writing from his knowledge of what contemporary Jews did at Passover? Sadly, we lack conclusive evidence.

HAROSET IN THE TALMUDS

Both Talmuds contain tractates that expand on Mishna Pesaḥim and provide more detail about haroset. Many later concepts of haroset look back to the talmudic discussions, particularly those in the Babylonian Talmud.

Haroset in the Jerusalem Talmud

In a passage from around the fifth century, the Jerusalem Talmud adds to the description of the Seder in the Mishna, which had specified the special foods brought before the leader of the Seder, including haroset. It now discusses an alternative name for haroset, its texture and its symbolism:

> They bring before [the leader of the Seder] unleavened bread (matza) and bitter lettuce (*ḥazeret*) and the haroset…
>
> The people of the house of Issi [said] in the name of Issi: "And why is [haroset] called by the name of *dukkeh*? Because she pounds (*dakhah*) [it] with (him/them/it) [corrupt text]."
>
> R. Joshua b. Levi said: "It must be thick. That is, in memory of clay."
>
> Another *Tanna* teaches: "It must be soft [or runny]. That is, in memory of blood." (Y. Pesaḥim 37d)

---

10. A. Dalby, *Food in the Ancient World from A to Z* (London, 2003), 118; 212, who quotes Athenaeus ii 63d–64f. See also ix 367c–368c. *Bulbusin* (=*bolboi*) appear in the talmudic literature. See Y. Feliks, *Tractate Shevi'it*, vol. 2 (Jerusalem, 1986), 451–3, who also identifies them in Y. Demai 22c. *Bolboi* are still eaten in rural Greece and Italy: A. F. Buccini, "The Bitter – and Flatulent – Aphrodisiac: Synchrony and Diachrony of the Culinary Use of *Muscari Comosum* in Greece and Italy," in *Vegetables: Proceeding of the Oxford Symposium on Food and Cookery 2008*, ed. S. R. Friedland (Totnes: Prospect Books, 2009), 46–55.

Having listed haroset among the special foods, the Jerusalem Talmud notes that haroset is called *dukkeh,* and asks why. The answer given is that this is because it is pounded (*dukhah*). It is interesting to note that the Vilna Gaon, the famous eighteenth-century Rabbi Elijah of Vilna, wrote about the use of the root D-V-KH, from the verb meaning "to pound," in his description of making haroset.[11] He saw it as an allusion to the manna, which the Children of Israel pounded in a mortar (*medokhah*) before baking: "*Dakhu bamedokhah*" (Num. 11:7–9). The Torah tells us that manna, the miraculous total food that fell from heaven, was as sweet as "wafers with honey." It was provided by God after the Exodus from Egypt, and throughout the forty years His people remained in the wilderness (Ex. 16:1–36). Thus, for the Vilna Gaon at least, there is an allusion in the haroset to the mercy of God, symbolized as a sweet heavenly food.

The name *dukkeh* for haroset has survived to the present day. Jews from Yemen – who were cut off for many centuries from other Jewish communities, and had no access to the Babylonian Talmud – relied on the Jerusalem Talmud as their religious authority. To this day, the Yemenite Jewish community in Israel calls haroset *dukkeh.* (When Naomi Gozi gave me her mother Hamama's recipe for haroset, found in chapter 6, she noted specifically that the Yemenites still call it *dukkeh.*)

Yemenite Jews also have an interesting interpretation of another aspect of haroset. I noted that the Jerusalem Talmud text above was corrupt. It can be read to say that "it (a feminine pronoun referring to haroset) is pounded with it (a masculine pronoun, referring to the bitter herbs)," and some medieval rabbis, in fact, recommended making haroset with pounded bitter herbs. But other rabbis, and in particular those of Yemenite origin, read the passage as "She pounds with him," and say that a husband and wife should make haroset together.[12]

---

11. Rabbi Elijah ben Solomon Zalman of Vilna (1720–1797), *Biurei Aggadot* on Berakhot 57b (Jerusalem: unknown publisher, 1971), 45.

12. See on this the authoritative Yemenite rabbi in his edition of the Passover Haggada: Y. Kappah, ed., *Sefer Aggadeta DePisha* (Jerusalem: HaAguda LeHatzalat Ginzei Teiman, 1958).

The Jerusalem Talmud goes on to discuss the texture of haroset. R. Joshua b. Levi, a third-century rabbi from the Land of Israel, is quoted as saying that the haroset must be thick like mud or clay. Haroset with this texture would thus evoke the clay used by the Children of Israel for making bricks, described in the Book of Exodus, when they were slaves to Pharaoh in Egypt. The anonymous *Tanna*, however, disagrees, teaching that haroset should be soft (or runny) "in memory of the blood." It is unclear what blood this recalls. Blood from the Passover lamb was used by the Jews to mark their houses before they left Egypt. They dipped bunches of the pungent herb called hyssop into it and painted it on the lintels of their houses as a sign for the Destroyer to *pass over* them and spare their children (Ex. 12:21–3). However, the blood may also refer to the first of the Ten Plagues in the Book of Exodus, during which all the water in Egypt turned to blood (Ex. 7:20f.). (Later generations saw more sinister associations of haroset with blood.) Thus the Jerusalem Talmud has two competing symbolisms for haroset: clay and blood, both memories of different aspects of the Egyptian slavery.[13]

Haroset in the Babylonian Talmud

The Babylonian Talmud, finalized around the seventh century, first expands upon an earlier statement in Mishna Pesaḥim 10:3, which discusses dipping the bitter lettuce, but does not specify what it is dipped into:

> Rav Pappa said, "This lettuce, you must plunge it in the haroset, because of *kappa*..."
>
> [But others disagree:] "You do not need to plunge it in, because *kappa* is destroyed by the smell"...
>
> Rav Pappa also said, "A person should not leave the bitter herbs (*maror*) in the haroset, just in case the sweetness of the spice destroys its bitterness." (Pesaḥim 114a–116a)

---

13. These were finally reconciled in the Middle Ages by the Tosafist Rabbi Jacob ben Judah Hazan MiLondres, *Etz Ḥayim*, ed. I Brodie (Jerusalem: Mosad HaRav Kook, 1962–67), as we shall see in chapter 3.

R. Pappa, a Babylonian rabbi of the fourth century, often appears in talmudic discussions of food (he is also reported to have been a fat man).[14] According to him, the lettuce used as bitter herbs contained a harmful element known as *kappa*. It is unclear from the text precisely what *kappa* is. Various medieval commentators explained it as unhealthy juices or some form of insect. But it may also have been an evil spirit. Later in the talmudic text, we hear of antidotes to *kappa* in different vegetables: "The *kappa* of lettuce is counteracted by radishes, the *kappa* of radishes by leeks, the *kappa* of leeks by hot water; the *kappa* of all these by hot water." These would make *kappa* sound like harmful juices, were it not for the cryptic spell offered by the Talmud if you have no *kappa* antidote handy: "Let him say thus: *kappa*, *kappa*, I remember you and your seven daughters and eight daughters-in-law" (Pesaḥim 116a). This makes *kappa* sound more like a demon or an evil spirit. Later kabbalistic rabbis gave all sorts of symbolic meanings to the mother with her seven daughters and eight daughters-in-law, but these need not detain us here.[15] I should just note that the Babylonian Talmud is very often particularly concerned with demons and spirits, so this may be a later Babylonian addition, rather than part of the earlier concepts.[16]

R. Pappa, then, believes that the bitter herbs should be dipped in the haroset in order to counteract the *kappa*, but he specifies that they should not be left there, as this would destroy their bitterness. Presumably, this opinion is the origin of the custom among present-day Jews who came from Germany not to eat haroset at all. They merely dip the bitter herbs and then eat them, after shaking off any haroset adhering to them.[17]

---

14. In antiquity, when many people subsisted just above starvation, being fat was regarded as an advantage. But see also: D. Boyarin, "The Talmud as a Fat Rabbi: A Novel Approach," *Text & Talk* 5 (2008): 603–19.
15. *Biurei Aggadot* (above, n. 11), 44–5.
16. See G. Bohak, *Ancient Jewish Magic* (Cambridge: Cambridge University Press, 2008).
17. Informants: Prof Aharon Oppenheimer; Ruti Rosenblatt (below, chapter 6), and see: https://www.koltorah.org/halachah/the-mitzvah-of-charoset-by-rabbi-chaim-jachter (accessed April 2018).

The Babylonian Talmud then turns to the statement of the Mishna about bringing matza, bitter lettuce and haroset to the leader of the Seder, discussed in the Jerusalem Talmud:

> R. Shimi bar Ashi said: "[You should put] matza in front of each one [of the participants at the Seder], *maror* (bitter herbs) before each one, and haroset before each one"...
>
> But R. Huna said: "Each of these things [should be] in front of the one who recites the Haggada."
>
> And the ruling is according to R. Huna. (Pesahim 116a)

Here the Babylonian rabbis are concerned with how many portions of matza, bitter herbs and haroset were required at the Seder, and they rule that only one was necessary, for the leader of the Seder. They then carry on to consider whether haroset is a mitzva, citing the mishna we have seen with R. Elazar b. Tzadok's evidence. Finally, they come to the question, debated in the Jerusalem Talmud, of what haroset signifies. Their version differs somewhat:

> What is the mitzva?
>
> R. Levi says, "In memory of the apple."
>
> But R. Yohanan says, "In memory of the clay."
>
> Abbaye says, "Therefore you have to make it acidic and to make it thick." (Pesahim 116a)[18]

A number of midrashim and commentaries make it clear that the apple mentioned by R. Levi refers to a verse from the biblical Song of Songs (8:5): "I roused thee under the apple tree. There thy mother was in travail with thee; there she who bore thee was in travail." This apple tree

---

18. The printed versions of the Talmud have here: "Make it acidic, in memory of the apple. And you must make it thick in memory of the clay." This seems to be a comment by Rashi which got interpolated in the text, as it is missing in the manuscripts. See R. N. N. Rabbinowicz, *Dikdukei Soferim* (München: A. Huber, K. Hof Buchdrucker, 1874), vol. 6, on Pesahim 116a.

is also the subject of a beautiful midrash about the Children of Israel in Egypt, which I will look at more closely below.

R. Levi, we should note, does not actually say that apples should be included in the haroset, but it is clear that, for him, apples are a taste-memory, closely connected to haroset and its symbolism. R. Yohanan, on the other hand, like R. Joshua b. Levi in the Jerusalem Talmud, believes that haroset is in memory of the clay used for the bricks that the Jews made as slaves in Egypt. We should note here that R. Yohanan and R. Levi are both rabbis from the Land of Israel, so the Babylonian Talmud here may be reporting a debate that actually took place there but was not preserved in Land of Israel sources.

What is to be done with these differing opinions? The Babylonian Talmud cites Abbaye, a fourth-century Babylonian rabbi, who says that haroset must be *both* acidic and thick. Apples clearly were more sour than sweet in late antique Babylonia, and probably much more sour in antiquity in general than they are today. The first-century Roman writer Pliny writes of apples, including the Italian wild apple, "with a horrible sourness...so powerful it will blunt the edge of a sword."[19] Thus Abbaye makes his haroset acidic in memory of the apples.

The Babylonian Talmud proceeds with a text that supports first R. Yohanan's opinion, and then R. Elazar b. Tzadok's ruling that haroset is a mitzva:

> There is a *baraita* like the statement of R. Yohanan: The spice is in memory of the straw, the haroset is in memory of the clay.
> R. Elazar b. Tzadok said: "The merchants in Jerusalem used to say, 'Come take your spices for the mitzva.'"

The *baraita* confirms R. Yohanan's view that haroset is a memory of the clay, rather than of the apples. Further support for R. Yohanan comes from two medieval rabbis, who may have had a text of the Jerusalem Talmud that differed somewhat from the version with which we

---

19. Pliny, *Natural History* 15.52. There is some uncertainty as to whether the biblical *tapuaḥ* is indeed an apple or some other fruit: D. Zohary, M. Hopf, *Domestication of Plants in the Old World*, 3rd ed. (Oxford: Oxford University Press, 2000), 143–4; 171–4.

are familiar. Our texts of the Mishna and the Talmuds do not reveal where the name "haroset" came from. But both the *Roke'aḥ* and the *Mordekhai* [20] write that in the Jerusalem Talmud, in the chapter dealing with the Eve of Passover, it says, "Why was it called by the name of haroset? In memory of the bricks which were made from *ḥarsit.*" In another passage from the Jerusalem Talmud, *ḥarsit* is described as pale-colored earth from which pottery was made (Y. Shabbat 11b), a material clearly resembling clay. While the Babylonian Talmud associates haroset with apples then, it rejects the view that this is its major association. The apples may hint at the taste of haroset, but they are not mentioned as an ingredient. The important thing is that haroset should be thick like clay, and acidic, and that spices should be added, in memory of the straw (Ex. 5:6–18).

Straw was a critical element in the Israelites' brick making in Egypt according to the biblical account. When Moses asked Pharaoh to let his people go, his first response was to refuse, and to increase their suffering by cutting off their supply of straw, while still demanding the same number of bricks as before. The Israelites protested bitterly that Moses had simply made their lot worse: "The Lord look upon you and judge, because you have made our savour abhorrent in the eyes of Pharaoh and in the eyes of his servants" (Ex. 5:21).[21] By including spices in the haroset, in memory of the straw, the rabbis of the Talmud have changed the metaphorical abhorrent stink of the Israelite slaves to the sweet smell of the spices.

Spices were also used as part of the worship of God Himself in the incense offered at the Temple altar. So with the inclusion of spices, haroset became part of the celebration of redemption on Passover eve.

The texts here record the discussion of the multiple symbolic meanings of haroset, which serve to remind the participants in the Seder of various aspects of the deliverance of the Jews from slavery. But these symbolisms can be seen to be shifting over the years and miles which separate the sources of the Land of Israel, i.e. the Mishna and

---

20. For more about the *Roke'aḥ* (Rabbi Eleazar ben Judah of Worms [1165–1230]) and the *Mordekhai* (Rabbi Mordechai ben Hillel [c. 1240–1298]), see below, chapter 3.
21. Translation adapted as in JPS (1917) version.

the Jerusalem Talmud, from the Babylonian Talmud. Haroset is now a memory of the clay for the bricks of slavery, with the spices a memory of the straw. There is no longer any reference to the blood mentioned in the Jerusalem Talmud, but we now have the symbolism of redemption. Thus haroset is bivalent in its significance, and those who eat it are incorporating the memories of both slavery and redemption.

As I have noted, we do not know whether haroset belongs to the time of the Second Temple or to the later period after the destruction of the Temple. However, if haroset was taken into use after the Destruction, this would certainly reflect the talmudic tendencies to emphasize midrashim of comfort and the promise of redemption for a generation bereft of the Temple.

HAROSET AND THE GRECO-ROMAN WORLD

By the end of Temple times, when we first hear of haroset, the Land of Israel had long been under the influence of Greece and Rome. Is there any evidence of haroset or something like it in Greek or Latin literature?

While rejecting the religious cults of the Greeks and Romans, Jews lived their lives in the Greco-Roman world, and willingly or unwillingly took part in its culture. Their everyday language appears to have been Aramaic, but some of them spoke Greek as well, and many Greek words found their way into the texts of the Mishna and the Talmuds. King Herod built the Second Temple using Greek orders of architecture. And there is clear evidence from the Tosefta's description of a formal meal that at least some Jews in the Land of Israel dined like Greeks or Romans on occasion:

> What is the order of the meal? As the guests enter, they are seated on benches or chairs until everyone assembles.
>
> Once everyone has arrived, they give them [water] for their hands, and each one washes one hand.
>
> They mix [wine] for them in the cup, and everyone makes the blessing for himself. They bring them hors d'oeuvres, and everyone makes the blessing for himself.

They get up [on couches] and recline, and they bring them [water for washing] their hands, and even though each has already washed one hand, he now washes both hands.

They mix the cup for them, and even though each one has already said the blessing over the first, he says the blessing over the second. They bring them hors d'oeuvres, and although each one has made the blessing over the first, he makes the blessing over the second, but [now] one person makes the blessing for everyone.

Someone who arrives after three [courses] of hors d'oeuvres is not allowed to come in. (Tosefta Berakhot 4:8)

The description above of a formal, festive meal is, at the same time, like and unlike the Passover Seder. More than anything, it recalls the Greco-Roman meal called a *symposium*, with its formal ceremonies, where the participants reclined on couches, and ate, and drank, and talked. So we should not be surprised to find that the Jewish celebration of Passover, the Seder meal itself, has many similarities to Greco-Roman cultural practice.[22] A depiction of such a formal meal on a mosaic floor from Sepphoris in Galilee can be seen in the picture insert (image 1).

Both the Seder and the *symposium* were meals where the participants reclined on couches; where discussion of texts and of the foods eaten formed part of the conversation; where ritual wine pouring and wine drinking played an important part; which often began with appetizers such as lettuce and eggs; and which included dipping food into sauces.[23] A third-century mosaic from Antioch (present-day Antakya, in Turkey) depicts the elements of a meal in order, as we can see from another photograph in the insert (image 2). After a silver *trulla* (ladle)

---

22. See on this: S. Stein, "The Influence of Symposia Literature on the Literary Form of the Pesah Haggadah," *Journal of Jewish Studies* 8 (1957): 13–44; contra: B. Bokser, *The Origins of the Seder: The Passover Rite and Early Rabbinic Judaism* (Berkeley: University of California Press, 1984); D. Smith, *From Symposium to Eucharist: The Banquet in the Early Christian World* (Minneapolis: Fortress Press, 2002).

23. On the *symposium* see in general: A. Dalby, *Siren Feasts: A History of Food and Gastronomy in Greece* (London/New York: Routledge, 1996; repr. 1997); on the Seder as *symposium*, see n. 22 above.

for hand washing comes the first course of eggs, artichokes and what is probably lettuce, served on a round flat silver plate together with a bowl of dipping sauce, with flat bread at the side. These images would certainly have reminded us of a Seder table, were it not for the accompanying pigs' feet.[24]

The Greco-Roman *symposium* with its servings of delicacies and philosophical discussions of foods was very much part of aristocratic culture. By adopting some of these aristocratic practices and bringing them into the home of every Jew, the rabbis were making even the poorest king for a day – a sensitive way of underlining the message of the redemption from Egypt and its foreshadowing of the redemption which was to come.

Aside from the general similarities between Seder and *symposium*, a number of scholars have suggested that there may be a specific connection between Greco-Roman sauces and haroset. Over fifty years ago, the scholar Siegfried Stein looked for haroset in Athenaeus' *Deipnosophists* (Philosophers at Dinner). This account of a Greek *symposium* from the third century CE was written in Egypt or Rome and was contemporary with the Mishna. Stein writes that dishes "similar though not identical to haroset" are described at length by the same author.[25] He defines haroset as being made of "nuts and fruits pounded together and mixed with spices, wine or vinegar."

Attempts to identify haroset solely on the basis of its modern ingredients, however, are doomed to failure. The ingredients, and hence the taste, have varied over time, and while almost all haroset today is sweet, we shall see this was not so in the past, nor were nuts an essential ingredient. We have already seen the Babylonian Talmud's reference to the acidic, or sour, taste of haroset. Athenaeus also cites an earlier Greek food writer, Archestratus, who gives instructions for dipping food into a sauce made of pounded hyssop and vinegar.[26] We shall see in the next

---

24. F. Cimok, ed., *Antioch Mosaics* (Istanbul: A Turizm Yayınları, 1995), 47.
25. Stein (above, n. 22), 16.
26. Archestratus of Gela was a fourth-century BCE food writer cited extensively by Athenaeus in his *Deipnosophists*. His most recent editors, Olson and Sens, describe *embapto* as "the *vox propria* (proper term) for dipping food in a side dish sauce or the like."

chapter that both hyssop and vinegar are present (among other things) in a recipe for haroset given by Maimonides (the Rambam) in the twelfth century.[27] Interestingly, a dry mixture of pounded hyssop, salt and spices is sold today in the modern Middle East as a dipping condiment for bread, or as a spread for dough before it is baked. This is called *dukkeh*.[28] We remember that this was the term used both in the Jerusalem Talmud and by present-day Yemenite Jews for pounded haroset.

If ingredients alone cannot provide the key to the origin of haroset, we must turn to philology and function. Perhaps surprisingly, some evidence for Greco-Roman haroset comes from Egypt in the Middle Ages. The Cairo Genizah, a collection of Jewish manuscripts, has preserved a fragment of a mishnaic glossary that explains Hebrew and Aramaic terms from the Mishna by using Greek words transliterated into Hebrew characters. This has been published by Nicholas de Lange, who dates it to "earlier than the tenth century," making it one of the earliest documents in the Genizah.[29]

In the glossary, the Hebrew words *"shafah haroset,"* "pounds haroset," are translated into Greek and transliterated into Hebrew letters as טריבי אנבמוס, *tribei enbamous*. *Enbamous* appears to refer to the Greek word *embamma*, which means a dipping sauce, deriving from the verb *embapto*, to dip. As noted above, Archestratus also mentions dipping (*embapte*) food; his particular sauce was made of pounded hyssop and vinegar.[30] Clearly, however, not all forms of *embamma* were made with hyssop and/or vinegar. The Roman author Pliny, for example, mentions a form of *embamma* made with mint (*NH* 20.53.147).

I have already mentioned the New Testament account of Jesus at the Last Supper dipping in the dish, identifiable, possibly, as haroset. It can hardly be coincidental that *embapto* is the verb used by Jesus in the

---

27. Maimonides, *Commentary on the Mishna*, Pesaḥim 10:3 *ad loc.*
28. *Dukkeh/dukkah*: C. Roden, *A New Book of Middle Eastern Food* (Harmondsworth: Penguin, 1985), 89–90.
29. N. de Lange, *Greek Jewish Texts from the Cairo Genizah* (Tübingen: Mohr Siebeck, 1996), 304 no.16, l. 12.
30. Archestratus, *Fragments from the Life of Luxury*, ed. and trans. J. Wilkins and S. Hill (Totnes: Prospect Books, 2011), 58, with Greek text in Athenaeus' *Deipnosophists* vii, 326f., which has *hyssopos*, like the Septuagint text of Exodus 12:22.

two Gospel accounts (Matt. 26:23, mentioned above; Mark 14:20) of the disciple who will dip (*embapsas, embaptomenos*) with him in the dish.

Additional evidence comes from the one Greco-Roman cookery book which has survived from antiquity. This collection, known as *de re coquinarea*, is attributed to the legendary Roman gourmet Apicius. In its present form it dates to fourth-century Rome, but it certainly includes earlier material from the first and second centuries CE. The Latin text often uses Greek words, in the same way that present-day English cookery writers aspiring to *haute cuisine* use French culinary terms. The collection includes two ways of dressing lettuce and endives:[31]

Endives and lettuces:
Correct endive with a dressing of *liquamen*,[32] a little oil and chopped onion. But instead of lettuce in winter serve endive in *enbamma* or with honey and sharp vinegar.

Lettuces: with *oxypor[i]um*, with vinegar and a little *liquamen* for the digestion, and to ease wind and *to prevent the lettuces from doing harm*. [Stresses in italics are mine.]

2 oz cumin,
1 oz ginger,
1 oz green rue,
12 scruples (=½ oz) juicy dates,
1 oz pepper,
9 oz honey,
Ethiopian, Syrian or Libyan cumin.

Pound the cumin after you have steeped it in vinegar. When it has dried, mix all the ingredients with the honey. When required, mix half a teaspoonful with vinegar and a little *liquamen* or take half a teaspoon after dinner.

---

31. Translation: C. Grocock, S. Grainger (eds. and trans.), *Apicius: A Critical Edition with an Introduction and an English Translation of the Latin Recipe Text* (Totnes: Prospect Books, 2006), iii, 18, 1–2, slightly adapted.
32. *Liquamen* was the famous Roman salty fish sauce also known as *garum*.

The recipes here specify that these dips "correct" (*medere*) endives. They state that lettuce and endives are interchangeable, and can be served either with *enbamma*, or honey and vinegar.[33]

The digestive sauce called *oxyporium*, noted specifically for *preventing lettuce doing harm*, is reminiscent of the Babylonian Talmud's haroset, which counteracted the harmful *kappa* in the bitter herbs. Talmudic bitter herbs, as I have noted, were also usually lettuce or endives.

Greek and Roman doctors such as Galen and Anthimus usually saw lettuce as beneficial, or at least less harmful than other vegetables. Athenaeus, writing about the Greek *symposium*, suggests that lettuce is an anti-aphrodisiac. It has been claimed that these supposed anti-aphrodisiac properties encouraged the use of lettuce at the Seder; the rabbis wished to discourage the riotous revelry common at Greek *symposia* after the banquet.[34] However, it may be noted that lettuce was often eaten as an appetizer by Greek and Roman banqueters with no apparent concern about its possible effect on their subsequent sexual function.[35]

Although both the Talmud and the *Apicius* collection agree on the potential harmfulness (or at least bitterness) of lettuce and endives, and both discuss the powers of haroset and *enbamma* (and *oxyporium*) to correct this potential harm, we are not told of the ingredients of *enbamma* or haroset. However, we shall see that many of the ingredients mentioned in the *Apicius oxyporium* sauce – dates, as well as ginger, cumin, pepper, vinegar and honey – appear in various forms of haroset. Indeed, dates and date honey (*silan*) are ingredients of the earliest forms of haroset for which we have recipes, from the ninth and tenth centuries, as we shall see in chapter 2.

On the other hand, I have never seen rue – an ingredient of *oxyporium* – in a recipe for haroset, although herbs in general are sometimes mentioned. It may be relevant to note that the intensely bitter rue is a particular favorite with *Apicius*, appearing in about 20 percent of his recipes, which could reflect individual preference rather than common

---

33. One of the manuscripts of the *Apicius* collection here has the form *enbamma* like the Genizah glossary, rather than the classical Greek *embamma*.
34. Bokser (above, n. 22).
35. Athenaeus, *Deipnosophists* iii, 101b.

practice. There was, however, a trend of incorporating bitter herbs into haroset both in Ashkenaz and Sepharad in the Middle Ages. The vinegar added later to the mix recalls the vinegar or sour wine that was often added to haroset from the time of the *Geonim*, giving it a sweet-and-sour or even entirely sour taste.

We have seen that the Jerusalem Talmud called haroset *dukkeh*, indicating a food that was pounded. The Greek mishnaic glossary we saw above also indicates that haroset was pounded. The *embamma* described by Archestratus above was made of pounded hyssop and vinegar, and Apicius' *oxyporium*, used to counteract the harmful effects of lettuce, includes the instruction to pound some of the ingredients.

The Babylonian Talmud was more distant in place and time from the Greco-Roman world than the Jerusalem Talmud, and belonged to a different culinary culture. However, the Babylonian Talmud does sometimes preserve and cite older original material that has been lost from its Land of Israel counterpart. The Babylonian Talmud's discussion about haroset begins by citing rabbis from the Land of Israel, which implies that haroset originated in the Land of Israel. It is probable, then, that haroset owes its origins to the Greco-Roman dipping sauces whose function was to counteract the bitterness and/or ill effects of lettuce and endives. These sauces were made, at least sometimes, like haroset, by pounding some of the ingredients, and some of these ingredients overlap with known ingredients of haroset, even if they are documented from later dates. The philological evidence of the Genizah glossary confirms that some early medieval Jews identified haroset with the dipping sauce known to the Greco-Roman world by the Greek name of *embamma*.[36]

Bitter herbs appear to have been eaten on Passover from biblical times. However, in the Greco-Roman period, bitter lettuce and endives were identified as harmful, by some authorities at least, and in need of correction in a dipping sauce. Could this have been the reason for the introduction of haroset into the Passover Seder? Perhaps. Once it was

---

36. *Embamma* is also used as a term for haroset by the eighteenth-century Italian Christian Hebraist Antonio Zanolini in his *Lexicon Chaldaico-Rabbinicum* (Padua: Typis Seminarii, 1747), 263, s.v. *maror*.

there, however, the rabbis seem to have had no choice but to give it symbolic significance as well.

"UNDER THE APPLE TREE":
HAROSET AND THE MIDRASH

Rabbi Levi, in the Babylonian Talmud, suggested that haroset was "in memory of the apple." Apples have been an important element of Ashkenazic haroset from the Middle Ages to the present day, so I digress deliberately here to look at what the apple tree symbolized for the rabbis of late antiquity, particularly in the midrashim, the rabbinic explanations and parables on the biblical Song of Songs. The talmudic halakhic (legal) texts discussed haroset and its texture and taste, and these discussions became the basis for later rabbinical instructions of how to make it and use it. In parallel, the midrashic texts with their rabbinical interpretations of biblical texts, and especially their allegorizing tendencies, became the basis for many of the later rabbinical interpretations of what haroset symbolizes.

"The Song of Songs which is Solomon's" (Song. 1:1) is a series of love songs which include some of the most beautiful descriptions of the coming of spring to the Land of Israel. The rabbis debated whether to include these erotic poems into the canon of the Bible, but eventually accepted the view that "all the Writings are holy but the Song of Songs is the Holy of Holies."[37] So the Song of Songs is read aloud in synagogue on Passover, the spring festival.

The Song of Songs talks of many fruits and spices, as well as wine, milk and the finest oil. The fruits appear both growing, in fields, orchards and gardens, and as ready to be eaten. Thus there are vineyards and vines with tender grapes, green figs forming on the fig tree, an orchard of pomegranates in bloom, gardens of luscious fruits and nut trees. The lover rouses his beloved "under the apple tree," where her mother gave birth to her (8:5). Fruits ready to eat include raisin cakes and clusters of grapes, fragrant apples, pomegranates split open or giving their juice, and date honey.

---

37. Statement of Rabbi Akiva in Mishna Yadayim 3:5.

The lover compares his beloved to a date palm, with its clusters her breasts, and says, "I will go up into the palm tree" (7:8). Spices and perfumes adorn the lover and his beloved: "Nard and saffron, calamus (*kaneh*)[38] and cinnamon, with all trees of frankincense; myrrh, and aloes, with all the chief spices (*roshei besamim*)" (4:14). Spices also flavor their wine, and the Song ends with the lover asking his beloved to make haste to the "mountains of spices" (8:14).

Having accepted the Song of Songs into the Bible, the rabbis interpreted this love poetry allegorically: the lover is God and the Jewish people, His beloved. This interpretation is developed in a number of Midrashim, one of which, Song of Songs Rabba, was written in the Land of Israel, probably around the sixth century.

Many of the fruits and spices of the biblical love poem are explained as allegories of God and His love for the Jewish people, and of the Temple in Jerusalem where Jews had loved and worshipped Him. Thus the Midrash explains the very first mention of spices as referring to the incense used in the Temple at Jerusalem.[39] In the wilderness, the priests had taken the "best spices" (*besamim rosh*), including flowing myrrh (*mordror*) and cinnamon, for anointing the Tabernacle and its contents, and other spices for the incense (Ex. 30:23–38). The Babylonian Talmud gives us details of the traditions about the ingredients of the incense used in the Temple – and many of these spices are indeed the same as those mentioned in the Song of Songs: frankincense, nard, saffron, cinnamon and myrrh.[40]

Some of the fruits mentioned in the Song of Songs are also related to Temple worship. The fig tree laden with green figs is seen as being

---

38. *Kaneh* has not been identified: since the word in a non-spice context simply means a reed, fragrant reed is the literal meaning. The traditional translation, sweet calamus, is probably incorrect: M. Meyerhof, ed., trans. and com., *Sarh Asma al-Uqqar* (*l'Explication des Noms de Drogues*): *Un Glossaire de Matière Médicale Composé par Maïmonide: Mémoires Présentés à l'Institut d'Égypte* 41 (Cairo: Imprimerie de l'Institut Française d'Archéologie Orientale, 1940), 164–5; A. Dalby *Dangerous Tastes: The Story of Spices* (London: British Museum Press, 2000; repr. 2002), 171 n. 3.

39. Song of Songs Rabba 1:2:1.

40. Keritot 6a. The memory of the scent of the incense in the Temple is preserved by the inclusion of this description into the synagogue liturgy on Sabbath morning.

like the baskets of first fruits taken to the Temple, while the vines with tender grapes recall the Temple drink-offerings.[41] A mosaic from the synagogue in Sepphoris in Galilee depicting these first fruits can be seen in the picture insert (image 3).

Apart from memories of the Temple, the rabbis were also, indeed even more, concerned with God's eternal love for His people Israel, and with past and future redemption. So each of the fruits and blossoms of the Song of Songs in turn is interpreted by the Midrash as showing the love of God, the virtues of His beloved people and redemption past and in the future. The love of God for His people as His children is expressed through the gift of fruits and spices. Here is one example:

> *My beloved is gone down into his garden* (6:2) – God is like a king who had a garden where he planted rows of nut trees and apple trees and pomegranates. He handed them over to his son saying, "I do not require anything of you, only when these trees yield their first fruit bring it to me and let me taste, so I may see the work of my hand and rejoice in you."

The fruits are also allegorized as individual gifts given by God to His people, the most important of which was the Torah. The apple tree is compared to Mount Sinai where the Torah was given:

> *I roused thee under the apple tree* (8:5) – This refers to Sinai. Why is it compared to an apple tree? Because just as an apple tree gives fruit in the month of Sivan, so the Torah was given in Sivan.[42]

The commentaries on the Torah, the Mishna and Talmud are seen as the choice products of the fruits: the Talmud is "flavored" with the Mishna, like wine flavored with spices.[43] The fruits are also used as allegories for the People of Israel and their righteousness in praising God and studying His law:

---

41. Song of Songs Rabba 2:13:3.
42. Apples: Song of Songs Rabba 8:5:1.
43. Wine: Song of Songs Rabba 6:2:3; 8:2:1.

I went down into the garden of nuts (6:11) – this is the world. *To see the fruits of the valley* – these are Israel. *To see whether the vine had blossomed* – these are the synagogues and the houses of study. *Whether the pomegranates were in flower* – these are the children who are busy learning Torah and sit in rows like pomegranate seeds.

However the rabbis were nothing if not realistic, and there is a clear sense that the Jewish people includes both learned and ignorant, virtuous and less virtuous. Thus there are alternative explanations of *I went down into the garden of nuts.* For example:

I went down into the garden of nuts – just as the shell of a nut protects its fruit, so the ignorant of Israel strengthen those who study Torah.

or:

I went down into the garden of nuts – just as there are soft nuts, medium nuts and hard nuts, so in Israel there are those who give charity unsolicited, those who have to be asked before they give and those who do not give at all.[44]

Thus in the Midrash on the Song of Songs, the Jewish people is associated allegorically with a number of fruits, with the pomegranates, grapes, figs and dates which are part of the Seven Fruits of the Land of Israel (Deut. 8:8),[45] but also with apples and nuts.

The Midrash also alludes to redemption, memories of the past and hopes for the future. "For, lo, the winter is past" (2:11) was seen as an allusion to the four hundred years of slavery in Egypt, ended by God's mercy with the redemption at Passover. Hopes for the future redemption are expressed through the pomegranates: "*Thy shoots are an orchard of pomegranates* (4:13) – God will make Israel like an orchard of pomegranates in the messianic era."[46]

---

44. Nuts: Song of Songs Rabba 6:11:1.
45. "A land of wheat, and barley, and vines, and fig trees and pomegranates, a land of olive oil and [date] honey."
46. Redemption from Egypt: Song of Songs Rabba 2:11:1. Future redemption: 4:12:6.

More allegories of the apple tree are to be found in the midrashim on the biblical Book of Exodus, which tells the story of the first Passover and how God saved the Israelites from slavery in Egypt. The writers of the midrash weave the apple tree into the biblical Exodus narrative, using the verse we saw above from the Song of Songs – "I roused thee under the apple tree" (8:5) – and expanding on it. The Book of Exodus told how the Egyptian authorities had declared that all male Jewish babies were to be killed. In response, the midrash tells us, Israelite couples separated so as not to have babies who would be killed. Miriam, Moses' older sister, is reported to have pointed out to her parents that this way there would be no baby girls either, and the people would not survive. Her mother, Yocheved, was persuaded, and eventually gave birth to Moses, whom she hid in the bulrushes next to the River Nile (Ex. 2:21–3). Not to be outdone, the midrash tells us, other Israelite women followed her footsteps and seduced their husbands under the apple trees. Their babies too were hidden and saved:

> As soon as they had conceived they returned to their homes, and when the time of childbirth arrived they went out into the fields and gave birth beneath the apple tree, as it is said: "I roused thee under the apple tree; there thy mother was in travail with thee" (Song. 8:5). God then sent down an angel, who washed and beautified the babies like a midwife.... He also provided them with oil and honey to suck.[47]

The apple tree, then, became intimately associated with the Passover narrative, and in particular with God's mercy. We saw earlier that R. Levi said that haroset is in memory of the apple. Some of the medieval commentators on this passage saw that it must have been this sort of allegorical interpretation that R. Levi was referring to. The apple tree became a symbol of God's care for His people when they were slaves in Egypt, and haroset was taken to be a memory of that time. Later rabbis followed in R. Levi's footsteps and also related their haroset to the Song of Songs.

---

47. Exodus Rabba 1:12:4 with parallels in Land of Israel midrashim and Sota 11b, among others.

Chapter 2

From Babylonia to Cairo via Cordoba: The Beginning of Sephardic Haroset

"Do they have cloves in Aunt Yaffa's version?"

"…In her version? No. I don't know. I don't think so."

"What do they have?"

"They have…" she rehearsed it to herself, "…apples, nuts, honey…." She frowned. "Dates," she said. "Figs and dates. And that is what makes it different."

"Dates," the girl said.

"And it is more of a…'cake,' not a 'cake,' a…"

"…It's thicker," the girl said.

David Mamet, *Passover*

In David Mamet's short story *Passover*, a little girl and her grandmother are making haroset together.[1] Aunt Yaffa's thicker version of

---

1. D. Mamet, *Passover* (New York: St Martin's Press, 1995).

haroset is "the Sephardic kind," made with dates. We shall soon see that from the earliest records, Sephardic haroset was typically thick and made with dates. Where did Sephardic haroset originate, and how did it develop?

THE BABYLONIAN *GEONIM* AND THEIR HAROSET

After the completion of the Babylonian Talmud, leadership of the yeshivas, the academies of Jewish learning, in Babylonia was taken over by rabbis called the *Geonim*. One of the first of these was Rav Amram Gaon, who headed the important yeshiva at Sura in the ninth century. Rav Amram was the author and compiler of a Siddur, a prayer book (which is somewhat confusingly called a *Seder*). Unlike modern Siddurs, Rav Amram's includes the text of the Passover Haggada with accompanying instructions.[2] He writes that "They bring before him [the leader of the Passover Seder] haroset – *ḥallika* – which we make in our part of the world from dates."

Rav Amram Gaon is clearly noting a local custom about the ingredients used to make haroset, also called *ḥallika*, implying that it is different from customs elsewhere. He does not say whether dates were the only ingredient. If they were, then this rabbi from Babylonia is differentiating himself from the view in the Babylonian Talmud that haroset should taste acidic, in memory of apples. Dates would presumably have made a thick paste, so Rav Amram appears to accept the view of R. Yohanan, as interpreted by Abbaye, that haroset should be thick, in memory of the clay.

If Sura was the Oxford or Harvard of Babylonian yeshivas, then Pumbedita, headed by Rav Saadia Gaon, was the Cambridge or Yale. Rav Saadia lived in various places around the Mediterranean, but eventually moved to Babylonia at the beginning of the tenth century. He was the author of an Arabic Siddur, which includes a commentary on the

---

2. E. D. Goldschmidt, ed., *Seder Rav Amram Gaon* (Jerusalem: Mosad HaRav Kook, 1971). The Hebrew word *"seder"* means "order"; the Passover Seder is the *order* of the ritual. In the title of the *Seder* of Rav Amram, the term is equivalent to Siddur, the prayerbook, and contains the *order* of prayers throughout the Jewish year, including the Passover Haggada. It was written in the ninth century but the earliest examples we have are from the fourteenth century, so changes could have been introduced into it.

"Under the Apple Tree" by Asia Katz illustrates the haroset midrash

[Image 1] Symposium meal from ancient Sepphoris (Zippori) in Galilee

[Image 2] Third-century mosaic from the "House of the Buffet Supper" in Antioch

[Image 3] First-fruit offering from the fifth-century synagogue at Sepphoris

[Image 4] Bird's Head Haggada: Pounding haroset

[Image 5] Pounding haroset with pestle and mortar in the Middle Ages

[Image 6] Haggada from Castille: Distributing haroset

[Image 7] Barcelona Haggada:
Distributing haroset balls in the Middle Ages

[Image 8] Yahudah Haggada: Preparing haroset

[Image 9] Second Nuremberg Haggada (property of David Sofer): Haroset with pears

Passover Haggada.[3] Saadia mentions using lettuce, or wild or cultivated endives, for bitter herbs, and then says that haroset should be made of dates, nuts and sesame, kneaded together with vinegar. His name for haroset, *ḥallik,* is similar to Rav Amram's. To this day Jews from Iraq call their haroset *ḥallek* and make it from dates, nuts and sesame.

Saadia Gaon was so influential that he appears to have authorized his local custom as the authentic Sephardic haroset. He, too, was presumably relying on the opinion of R. Yohanan – accepted by the Babylonian Talmud – that clay, rather than apples, is the most important association with haroset, and that consistency is more important than ingredients. However, with the addition of the acidic vinegar, he preserves Abbaye's opinion in the Babylonian Talmud as well. Vinegar is not usually present in modern Sephardic versions of haroset.

Neither of these two *Geonim* spells out the function or symbolism of haroset.

MEDIEVAL NORTH AFRICA AND SPAIN

Jews from the Babylonian Diaspora developed their own traditions. Having moved from Babylonia to North Africa, many of them were then forced to flee for their lives to Spain and eventually back to North Africa.

Among them was Rabbi Isaac ben Jacob, who lived in Fez in Morocco in the eleventh century and was also known as al-Fasi (Alfasi), the man from Fez, or the Rif, after his initials (Rabbi Isaac al-Fasi). He remained part of the intellectual tradition of the Babylonian *Geonim,* even when he was forced to flee to Spain at the end of his life. There he lived first in Cordoba, and later in the wholly Jewish town of Lucena. He wrote a major commentary on the Babylonian Talmud, which is still printed to this day in the better editions. There we find details of the Rif's haroset. Following the Talmud's teaching that haroset should contain spices in memory of the straw in the bricks, al-Fasi specifies, "like cinnamon and *sanbal* which are like straw."

---

3. Rav Saadia Gaon (882–942), *Siddur R. Saadia Gaon,* ed. I. Davidson, S. Assaf and B. I. Joel (Jerusalem: Ḥevrat Mekitzei Nirdamim, 1941), 134. This Siddur was very popular in Egypt and other Arabic-speaking lands, but was lost for hundreds of years. Happily, it was found in modern times, and translated into Hebrew.

Sanbal is Arabic for spikenard or nard, both of which appear in the Song of Songs. But al-Fasi notes that he includes them because of their straw-like consistency, and not their symbolism. Interestingly, neither of these spices seems to have been regularly used for food at this period, only for scent or wine.[4]

Maimonides, the Rambam (Rabbi Moses ben Maimon), perhaps the greatest of all rabbinical commentators, was born in Cordoba in Spain in 1135. He too was forced to move, and while al-Fasi had fled west from Fez to Cordoba, Maimonides, a century later, fled back east from Cordoba to Fez, and then on to Cairo, because of persecutions by the fundamentalist Almohad Moslems. While still in Spain, Maimonides began work on his important *Commentary on the Mishna*. This includes a discussion of haroset.[5]

Maimonides addresses the mishnaic and talmudic discussions about whether haroset is a mitzva. According to him, if haroset is a mitzva as R. Tzadok (clearly he is referring to R. Elazar b. Tzadok) claimed, eating it would require a blessing, like any religious commandment. Participants at the Seder would be required to say, "[Blessed are You, O God]…who has made us holy with His commandments and commanded us to eat haroset." However, he says, this is not the halakha, Jewish law: in other words, this is not done.

The Rambam goes on to provide the first real recipe for haroset:

> Haroset is a mixture which has in it acidity and something like straw in memory of the clay. We make it like this: Soak figs or dates and cook them and pound them till they get soft, and knead them with vinegar and put in spikenard or thyme or hyssop without grinding them.[6]

---

4. C. Grocock and S. Grainger, *Apicius: A Critical Edition with Introduction and English Translations* (Totnes: Prospect Books, 2006), 34.

5. Maimonides made a number of later alterations to his commentary on the Mishna, which are noted in the edition by Y. Kappah, *Mishna with Maimonides' Commentary* (Jerusalem: Mosad HaRav Kook, 1963 [Hebrew]), but apparently not to this section.

6. *Commentary on the Mishna*, Pesaḥim 10:3 *ad loc.*

Maimonides clearly refers back to the talmudic discussions on the taste, texture and symbolism of haroset. But he breaks new ground by then giving instructions on how to make it – by soaking, cooking and pounding the ingredients (he uses the verb *dukhin*, pound, like the Jerusalem Talmud) until soft, and then kneading and adding spices, without grinding them. Presumably the whole, unground spices and herbs are more like stalks of straw. He also expands the list of ingredients with the addition of fresh figs, and thyme or hyssop.

The hyssop is especially interesting. The biblical account of the Exodus specifies that bunches of hyssop were to be used by the Israelites to mark their doorposts with blood, so that the Destroyer would *pass over* them. The Jerusalem Talmud quoted an opinion that haroset was in memory of blood. Maimonides included this memory in his haroset, although he does not actually quote the source from the Jerusalem Talmud. Hyssop and vinegar were, as we saw, ingredients of Archestratus' Greek version of *embamma*, the dipping sauce identified as haroset in the glossary from the Cairo Genizah. Did Maimonides inherit a tradition, lost to everyone else, of using hyssop in haroset, or are these ingredients merely coincidental? There are many centuries between him and Archestratus, and it is impossible to know.

Years later in Cairo, when Maimonides wrote his Code of Laws, the *Mishneh Torah*, he revisited the question of whether haroset is a mitzva. Haroset, he writes there, is only a lesser religious obligation, based on "the authority of the Scribes." [7] He repeats that it is in memory of the clay or mud used by the Israelites in Egypt. And he now provides a revised recipe:

> And how do you make haroset? You take dates or dried figs, or raisins or something similar, tread on them and put vinegar in them, and spice them with spice, as in clay mixed with straw, and bring it to the table on Passover eve.

---

7.   Maimonides, *Mishneh Torah*, ed. M. D. Rabinowitz et al. (Jerusalem: Mosad HaRav Kook, 1957), *Zemanim* 2, *Hilkhot Ḥametz UMatzah*, vii, 11.

This new recipe is less detailed – and less exact. Having listed a number of fruits, it adds, "or something similar," leaving the readers to choose.

Maimonides clearly accepts R. Yohanan's opinion in the Babylonian Talmud that haroset is in memory of the clay. Thus the consistency of the haroset is its important feature. And in that case, the ingredients can be varied according to what is available. The Babylonian *Geonim*, as we saw, specified that their local custom was to use dates. Maimonides also used dates and other fruit. In his *Commentary on the Mishna*, he mentioned fresh figs. In the later *Mishneh Torah*, he lists "dates or dried figs, or raisins, or something similar." In addition, the fruit, which was cooked and pounded in the earlier text, is now no longer pounded but trodden on.

Evidence that this practice took place even in modern times comes from twentieth-century Iraq. As we shall see in chapter 6, I interviewed people from many communities about their haroset. Eveline Tufiq, who came from Iraq, remembered that dates for the haroset were trodden between palm leaves.

In the case of the spices, what is most important to Maimonides in the *Mishneh Torah* is that they recall the straw used in the clay. Thus he no longer specifies any particular spice, and gone are the "spikenard or thyme or hyssop." Maimonides also appears to accept Abbaye's conclusion that, in addition to having a clay-like consistency, haroset should be acidic. In the *Commentary on the Mishna*, he defined haroset as a food with a degree of acidity. In the *Mishneh Torah*, he does not mention acidity, but does specify that haroset is to be made with vinegar. The combination of the sweet fruits with vinegar will have produced a sweet-sour haroset.

Maimonides was not only a giant of Jewish learning – it was said of him that "from Moses [in the Bible] until Moses, there was none like Moses" – he was also a physician. One of his instructions for healthy living tells us that fresh fruits, particularly sour ones, are bad for us, as they attack the body "like swords."[8] Presumably this is why he made his haroset sour with vinegar, rather than sour fruit. And it may well have been why he recommended cooking the dates. The only fruits which

---

8.   *Hilkhot De'ot* 4:11.

are good fresh or dried, he says, are figs, grapes and almonds. Perhaps this is why he specified dried figs and raisins in this revised recipe in the *Mishneh Torah*.

An Arabic commentary on the Passover Haggada, attributed to Rabbi David ben Abraham, a grandson of Maimonides, who was a rabbi in Damascus in the thirteenth century, was recently translated into Hebrew from the single manuscript that survives.[9] Here we find Rabbi David's haroset recipe, which differs from both of his grandfather's recipes:

> How do you make haroset? You take raisins and gourds and dates pressed well, and sesame and almonds and crush them all. And you add to them mint (*nana*) to improve their taste, knead them in vinegar so that it will remain a little thick and be like clay. And you should add apple to it in memory of "I roused thee under the apple tree" (Song. 8:5). And also to remind us of the miracles which the Holy One blessed be He did for them in the wilderness, at the time of their birth, as we will make clear. And you should also add nuts in memory of "I went down into the garden of nuts" (Song. 6:11), which is an allusion to Egypt, for just as with nuts a man cannot eat the fruit until he has crushed them and made them fine, so Israel could not leave their slavery until the Egyptians were crushed and broken by the plagues and decimated, and only afterwards could they leave there. And you must also add a lot of spices like ginger and spikenard and cloves (*karanful*) and so on, in memory of the straw in the clay.[10]

Like Maimonides in the *Commentary on the Mishna*, Rabbi David gives detailed instructions. He, too, talks of pressing and crushing and

---

9. Rabbi David ben Abraham Maimuni, grandson of Maimonides (1222–1300), also called Rabbi David HaNagid, *Midrash on the Passover Haggada* (tr. from the Arabic by S. Barh"i Yerushalmi, Jerusalem; Wagshal, 1981 [Hebrew]), 37.

10. *Karanful*, the Arabic for cloves, modern French *girofle*: M Meyerhof, ed., trans. and com., *Sarh Asma al-Uqqar (l'Explication des Noms de Drogues): Un Glossaire de Natière Médicale Composé par Maïmonide: Mémoires Présentés à l'Institut d'Égypte* 41 (Cairo: Imprimerie de l'Institut Française d'Archéologie Orientale, 1940), 207.

kneading. But he is the first Sephardic rabbi, apparently, to have introduced apples into the mix (his Ashkenazic contemporaries had been
using apples for some time), incorporating Abbaye's teaching that haroset should be sour "in memory of the apple."

Rabbi David also includes some stranger ingredients, not present
in any other recipes I have found. Gourds (*delaat*) do not appear any-
where else, although there are greens (*yerakot*) – vegetables or herbs –
in some contemporary Ashkenazic recipes. Could the gourds serve the
function of providing cheaper bulk for the haroset? Or is this a scribal
error for some other more common ingredient?

A further question arises about the mint (*nana*) added "to
improve the taste," as once again, I am aware of no other haroset with
mint. However, Maimonides did list hyssop and thyme in his earlier
recipe. Is mint his grandson's nearest local approximation in Damascus? Mint was indeed an ingredient in Pliny's *embamma* (*HN* 20.53.147),
and it also appears in the Babylonian Talmud, albeit not in a Passover
context. It was also a flavoring popular with medieval Arab cooks, some
of whom were Rabbi David's contemporaries. The thirteenth-century
Kitāb Waṣf al-aṭ'ima al-mu'tāda, the *Description of Familiar Foods* from
Baghdad, has a recipe for raisins and mint, *zabīb wa-na'na'*, in the section on pickles and condiments. It too contains vinegar and spices. The
fourteenth-century cookbook from Egypt, the *Kanz al-fawā'id fī tanwī'
al-mawā'id*, includes an electuary, *ma'jūn al-na'nā'*, a medicinal powder
based on mint and mixed with honey.[11]

We saw that Saadia Gaon's haroset contained nuts, although there
was no explanation or symbolism given for them. Rabbi David, on the
other hand, gives the nuts a symbolic rationale, relying on a verse from
the Song of Songs. Just as the apple tree is a midrashic allusion to the

---

11. Mint in medieval Arab recipes: M. Rodinson, A. J. Arberry and C. Perry, *Medieval
Arab Cookery* (Totnes: Prospect Books, 2001), 395; N. Nasrallah, *Treasure Trove of
Benefits and Variety at the Table: A Fourteenth-Century Egyptian Cookbook* (Leiden/
Boston: Brill, 2018), 268.

M. Sokoloff, *A Dictionary of Jewish Babylonian Aramaic in the Talmudic and Geonic
Periods* (Ramat Gan: Bar Ilan University Press, 2002), 751; 756 has recently called
into question some of the Babylonian Talmud references to mint and suggested it
might be referring to *Ammi copticum* (*ajwan*).

Jewish people's slavery and redemption in Egypt, so the garden of nuts is a reference to the Jews in Egypt. In our text of Songs of Songs Rabba and other Midrashim,[12] the nuts which are trodden on symbolize Israel, who survives all persecutions, and whose sins are thus atoned for. In a typically rabbinic euphemistic transformation, Rabbi David changes the midrash. Clearly, he did not want to mention the possibility that Israel might be crushed, so he adjusted the symbolism to represent the crushing of the oppressors instead.

Rabbi David's spices are interesting too. He lists spikenard like his grandfather and al-Fasi, but not cinnamon. Instead, he includes ginger and cloves (*karanful*). We shall see that both ginger and cloves were very popular with his Ashkenazic contemporaries.

Finally, in this survey of early Sephardic commentators I return to Spain, this time to Gerona, to the fourteenth-century Rabbenu Nissim ben Reuben Girondi, known as the Ran. The Ran wrote a supercommentary on the talmudic commentary of al-Fasi. Although he lived and wrote in Spain, Sepharad, he was a pupil of Rabbi Moses ben Nahman (Nahmanides or the Ramban), who was heavily influenced by the Ashkenazim of northern France. His haroset reflects this influence.

In his commentary on the text in Tractate Pesaḥim of the Babylonian Talmud, the Ran quotes the midrash about the apple tree and its connection to Egyptian slavery (as Rabbi David, the grandson of Maimonides, had done). He goes on to add that the haroset must be acidic, with the addition of various acidifiers such as apples and vinegar; and thick, in memory of the clay. He does not mention any other ingredients, particularly the dates we have become familiar with from all other Sephardic writers on haroset. Rabbi David had included apples in his recipe for Sephardic haroset, but only as one ingredient among many, and together with dates. In the Ran's haroset, they are a main ingredient. We shall see that sour, apple-based haroset is indeed much more typical of Ashkenaz.

---

12. Song of Songs Rabba 6:11; Exodus Rabba 36; Ḥagiga 15b.

HAROSET FROM THE BORDER LANDS

Provence

The border lands between Sepharad and Ashkenaz – Italy and Provence – were home to flourishing Jewish communities in the Middle Ages, which developed their own traditions of haroset.

The Jewish traveler Benjamin of Tudela in Spain left a record in Hebrew of his travels all over the Mediterranean in the twelfth century. Benjamin includes a first-hand account of the thriving Jewish community at Lunel in Provence, where there was a center of rabbinic studies, and several famous rabbis:

> From Montpellier it is four parasangs to Lunel, in which there is a congregation of Israelites, who study the Law day and night. Here lived Rabbenu Meshullam the great rabbi, since deceased, and his five sons, who are wise, great and wealthy, namely: R. Joseph, R. Isaac, R. Jacob, R. Aaron and R. Asher the recluse, who dwells apart from the world; he pores over his books day and night, fasts periodically and abstains from all meat. He is a great scholar of the Talmud. At Lunel live also their brother-in-law R. Moses, the chief rabbi, R. Samuel the elder, R. Solomon Hacohen and R. Judah the Physician, the son of Tibbon, the Sephardi. The students that come from distant lands to learn the Law are taught, boarded, lodged and clothed by the congregation, so long as they attend the house of study.[13]

Twelfth-century Lunel is also the source of another interesting recipe for haroset. A Hebrew manuscript, found in a library in St. Petersburg and known as *Teshuvot HaGeonim HaHadashot* (The New Responsa of the *Geonim*), contains previously unknown responsa of the Babylonian *Geonim* together with local Provençal material, some attributed and some anonymous.[14] One of these anonymous pieces is a recipe for haroset.

---

13. M. N. Adler, ed. and trans., *The Itinerary of Benjamin of Tudela* (London: H. Frowde, 1907; repr. New York: Feldheim, 1964): https://www.gutenberg.org/files/14981/14981-h/14981-h.htm#bpage_3 (accessed September 2018).

14. S. Emanuel, ed., *Teshuvot HaGeonim HaHadashot: MS. Moscow 566* (Jerusalem: Makhon Ofek, 1995), 50–1, sect. 40.

The manuscript contains a note, apparently from its compiler, mentioning Rabbi Abraham ben David of Posquières (Ravad) and "other sages of our time from Lunel." The Ravad lived in Lunel at the end of the twelfth century. The modern editor of the manuscript, Simcha Emanuel, suggests that it was compiled by one of his pupils, perhaps the well-known Rabbi Asher ben Meshullam, mentioned by Benjamin of Tudela.[15] Emanuel identified this Lunel recipe as being similar to that of *Sefer HaMenuḥa,* another Provençal work from later in the thirteenth century. Emanuel is undoubtedly correct, especially as both recipes contain a large quantity of chestnuts, which did not grow in Babylonia, but were widely available and cheap in southern France and northern Italy. So we can probably date this haroset to the end of the twelfth century or, at the latest, to the early years of the thirteenth.

The haroset from Lunel in the *Teshuvot HaGeonim HaḤadashot* is described as follows:

A reminder of how we make haroset on Passover:
To a third of a *hin*[16] of strong vinegar we add fruit:
   2 liters of white chestnuts, which should be cooked before grinding,
   2 liters of almonds, which should not be peeled,
   30 small dates or 10 large ones,
   800 nuts,
   50 medium apples or 30 large ones.
   And if you reduce the chestnuts and almonds and add [wal] nuts it will be better and nicer.

Of spices:
   half an ounce of ginger (*yeni bar*),
   half an ounce of spikenard (*sanbal*), which is called *ashpik,*

---

15. Rabbi Asher the ascetic is also called the Rosh of Lunel, to distinguish him from the better-known Rosh, Rabbi Asher ben Yehiel, whom we shall meet in the next chapter.
16. A *hin* is a biblical measure of volume. Some calculations put it at about four liters and others at seven liters. I was unable to find out how much it might have been thought to be in Rabbi Asher's days.

half an ounce of *kaneh,* which is called *canella,*
half an ounce of *teven mika,* which is called *ashkinant* (*Cym-bopogon schoenanthus*),
half an ounce of pepper.
And this amount is barely sufficient for us.

You should do it in this proportion, so that if you add to the third of a *hin,* you should also add some more of everything else, or if you reduce the vinegar, you should also reduce the rest of the ingredients proportionately. You should grind each of the different ingredients by itself with sixty apples, [grinding] each ingredient as is suitable for it, and afterwards you should further grind well all the ingredients together with the vinegar while holding the mortar (*medokhah*), so that the spices will be well ground with the vinegar, and you should mix them all up well.[17]

This unusually detailed recipe is not accompanied by remarks about the rationale for haroset or explanations of its symbolism. It is also remarkable for its huge quantities, which are "barely sufficient for us." Given the heading, "A reminder of how we make haroset on Passover," the recipe, preserved perhaps in a community archive, appears to have been intended for making haroset for the whole Jewish community of Lunel or for all the scholars studying there. This would fit in with Benjamin of Tudela's picture of a community that supplied food and clothing to all students who came from afar to study Torah.

It is clear that the recipe, introduced by the title, "How *we* make haroset," represents a purely local tradition. In addition to the huge quantities, there are many more details than we have encountered for making haroset. The proportions are seen as important, and there are instructions for adjusting them as well. The method, too, is not left to chance. The reader is told to grind each ingredient separately and then combine them all, and specifically to hold the mortar while pounding, so the spice will be well mixed with the vinegar. The word used here

---

17. *Teshuvot HaGeonim HaḤadashot* 40 (above, n. 14). It is unclear how many apples were used.

for mortar is *medokhah,* which recalls the Jerusalem Talmud's word for pounding haroset, *dukkeh.*

The recipe from *Teshuvot HaGeonim* is the first time we have come across chestnuts in haroset. It will become clear later that objections were raised to their use. Chestnuts often grew wild, and were thus free, or cost very little to buy. Many poor people in southern France and northern Italy subsisted on them as their staple food.[18] Perhaps the ascetic Rabbi Asher, the Rosh of Lunel, was among these.[19] In any event, using them as one of the major ingredients would bring down the price of haroset for the community, especially since imported spices were so costly. The recipe indeed mentions that substituting other nuts (presumably walnuts) for the chestnuts will "make it better and nicer.[20]

Let us look more closely at *Sefer HaMenuḥa* (The Book of Rest), with its similar recipe for haroset, written sometime between the end of the thirteenth century and the first half of the fourteenth century. It was written by Rabbi Manoah ben Simeon Badrashi,[21] who lived in Narbonne, a little southwest of Lunel in Provence. A commentary on Maimonides, the book was published in Constantinople. The play on the author's name and the title, Manoah/*Menuḥa*, underlines the authorship of the book.

Rabbi Manoah discusses Maimonides' haroset, and then adds his own comments. He wonders why we do not make a separate blessing over the haroset, and he answers by comparing haroset to the Four Species (*Arbaat HaMinim*) on the festival of Sukkot. Just as the rest of the Species are secondary to the palm branch (*lulav*), on which the blessing is recited, so is the haroset secondary to the bitter herbs, on which the blessing is recited.

---

18. Free wild chestnuts became an important food for Jews again in occupied France during the Second World War. See on this: J. Nathan, *Quiches, Kugel and Couscous: My Search for Jewish Cooking in France* (New York: Knopf, 2010), 340.
19. Benjamin of Tudela, *Itinerary*, 3 (above, n. 13).
20. The Hebrew word *egozim* is used for both nuts in general and walnuts in particular.
21. Rabbi Manoah ben Simeon Badrashi, *The Book of Rest* (*Sefer HaMenuḥa*) =Collection of Rishonim on Mishneh Torah 1 (*Kovetz Rishonim al Mishneh Torah*) (Jerusalem: unknown publisher, 1967), *Hilkhot Ḥametz UMatza*, vii, 11.

Rabbi Manoah also suggests a particularly local tradition, as he too begins his instructions with, "It is our custom." We have just seen the other, very similar haroset made with chestnuts from Lunel. Rabbi Manoah adds a few details about handling the ingredients: chestnuts are to be peeled, then pounded in a mortar; the thin skin is removed from the almonds, and they are pounded with a few walnuts; and the pips are removed from the raisins, before they are trodden with the figs and dates.

These ingredients are familiar to us by now, and it is interesting to see the continued stress on acidity from both sour apples and "strong wine vinegar." The fragrant reed, *kaneh bosem*, mentioned in the Song of Songs, and *teven misha/mika* are the same as in the recipe from Lunel, but the pepper is replaced with cloves, which Rabbi Manoah calls "nails of *kofer*" (the medieval French *girofle*). It is possible he associated this with the spice called *kofer* in the Song of Songs (1:14), although there it refers to henna, and not to cloves.[22] As we will see later in this chapter, spices in general were very expensive. Cloves, which were imported from the Moluccas, the Spice Islands, were especially costly, and they were considered exotic and desirable.

In spite of the similarities between the two recipes from *Teshuvot HaGeonim* and *Sefer HaMenuḥa*, there are differences. In Lunel, there were no figs or raisins, but there was pepper, rather than the more expensive cloves of *Sefer HaMenuḥa*.[23] The biblical *kaneh*, the fragrant reed, is identified in *Teshuvot HaGeonim* as *canella*, which evokes the French word for cinnamon – *cannelle*, called *kinamon* in Hebrew. Presumably, the identification with *kaneh* as *canella* is due to the similarity between the sounds of the names.

Both recipes name spices in Arabic, a trend that continued into later generations, as we shall see. Perhaps this was because some of the spice trade was in Arab hands and these names were common; perhaps

---

22. *Kofer* in Y. Feliks, *Spice, Forest and Garden Trees: Plants in Biblical and Rabbinic Literature*, vol. 2 (Jerusalem: Reuven Mas, 1997), 76–7. Feliks notes that this wrong identification is given in the medieval *Arukh* (for this work, see chapter 3).

23. Pepper lost its popularity as its price went down and it became part of the fare of ordinary people: P. Freedman, *Out of the East: Spices and the Medieval Imagination* (New Haven/London: Yale University Press, 2008), 43.

because both authors relied on earlier Jewish sources more subject to Arab influence, like Maimonides.

Joan Nathan, the modern cookery writer who has written about the food of French Jews, has adapted Rabbi Manoah's haroset for the modern Seder table:

> Gently pulse about 1 cup each cooked chestnuts, blanched almonds, raisins, figs and dates along with ¼ cup walnuts and one tart apple, peeled and quartered. Season with 1 teaspoon ground ginger and ¼ teaspoon ground cloves, and continue to pulse, adding enough wine vinegar (about 3 tablespoons) to reach the consistency of crunchy clay.[24]

There are no details here about peeling chestnuts or pipping raisins. Modern food preparation and packaging have rendered those activities unnecessary, and the food processor has replaced the laborious pounding and treading. The most obscure medieval spices are missing. The *kaneh bosem* and *teven misha* have very reasonably been replaced with ginger, which was a popular medieval spice.

Sefer Baalei HaAsufot (The Collectors' Book), a fragmentary collection of laws from the thirteenth century, provides a further haroset from Provence.[25] The book was probably written by Rabbi Judah ben Jacob Lattes from Carcassonne, a descendant, on his mother's side, of Rabbi Meshullam of Lunel.[26] Like some of his Ashkenazi contemporaries, the author included bitter herbs in his recipe for haroset (we will hear more about this in the next chapter). Rabbi Judah also expanded the list of spices, including *kaneh* and cinnamon, pepper, cloves (*naglens*), nutmeg or mace (*muskat*), and ginger. He associates all these with the spices of the Song of Songs. However, since a number of the spices

---

24. J. Nathan, *Quiches, Kugel and Couscous: My Search for Jewish Cooking in France* (New York: Knopf, 2010), 44.
25. On this manuscript published by M. Gaster, *Studies and Texts in Folklore, Magic, Medieval Romance, Hebrew Apocrypha and Samaritan Archaeology*, vol. 3 (London: Maggs Bros., 1923; repr. New York: Ktav, 1971), 221–7, see B. Z. Benedict, "Introduction to *Sefer Baalei HaAssufot*," *Sinai* 27 (1950 [Hebrew]): 322–9.
26. Benedict (above, n. 25), 326.

commonly used in his contemporary medieval Europe, such as pepper, cloves, ginger and nutmeg, are *not* mentioned in Song of Songs, Rabbi Judah includes them under the heading "all the chief (or best) spices" (*besamim rosh*). This phrase describes the spices used in the incense in the Tabernacle (Ex. 30:23), and the similar "chief of the spices" (*roshei besamim*) is found in the Song of Songs (4:14). Thus there is now a rationale for adding the more exotic and expensive cloves and nutmeg to the more common pepper, cinnamon and ginger. Nutmeg, which came from the Far East, was a novelty in Ashkenaz, and thus particularly sought after. It seems to have arrived in Palestine with the Arab conquest in the seventh century,[27] but it is not mentioned in French literature until the twelfth century or in English texts until the fourteenth, when Chaucer refers to *notemugge* together with *clowe-gilofre*, cloves.[28] Nutmeg remained desirable for hundreds of years, leading to bitter warfare over the distant islands in the Far East where it was grown. But that is not part of our story.[29]

Haroset in Italy

Rabbi Zedekiah ben Abraham Anav, who lived in Rome in the thirteenth century, also writes about making haroset. We do not know his exact dates, but in his book *Shibbolei HaLeket* (The Gleaned Ears) he mentions the burning of the Talmud in Paris in 1242.[30] His work, which codifies many religious laws, includes a commentary on the Passover Haggada, and he quotes both Sephardic and Ashkenazic authorities. Unfortunately, he does not specify his source for haroset.

Rabbi Zedekiah says there should be *yerakot,* herbs or vegetables, in haroset. However, he differs from everyone else I have found who has discussed haroset in including "blossoms from trees." Perhaps not very

---

27. Z. Amar, "Ibn al-Baytar and the Study of the Plants of Al-Sham," *Cathedra* 76 (1985): 49–76.

28. A. Dalby, *Dangerous Tastes: The Story of Spices* (London: British Museum Press, 2000), 54.

29. For warfare over the Moluccas, see G. Milton, *Nathaniel's Nutmeg: How One Man's Courage Changed the Course of History* (London: Hodder and Stoughton, 1999).

30. Rabbi Zedekiah ben Abraham Anav, *Shibbolei HaLeket*, ed. S. Buber (Vilna: Widow and Brothers Rom, 1886; repr. Jerusalem: Pe'er HaTorah, 1962), sect. 263, 184.

much fresh fruit was available in the Italian spring. Or maybe the tree blossoms evoke the images of flowers in the spring in the Song of Songs. A woman I met in the Jewish ghetto in Rome told me it is still the custom to add flowers, specifically rose petals, to present-day Roman haroset.

Rabbi Zedekiah, like many of his predecessors, follows Abbaye's view in the Babylonian Talmud that haroset should be acidic. In fact, he stresses this feature by calling his haroset by the vernacular name *aigros*, sour. (The word "vinegar" comes from *vin aigre*, sour wine.) Rashi, who came from northern France in the eleventh century, also called haroset *aigros*, so it is difficult to tell whether the *Shibbolei HaLeket* was relating to a French or Italian sour food.[31] Perhaps both possibilities are correct: we know from contemporary non-Jewish sources that sour tastes were popular all over Europe in the Middle Ages.[32] The *Shibbolei HaLeket* suggests as an example of acidic fruit, and possible ingredient of his haroset, "sharp apples," so that apples here are a recommended, rather than a necessary ingredient. Again, like his more northern contemporaries, Rabbi Zedekiah proposes cinnamon and spikenard as examples of spices.

But perhaps the most noteworthy ingredient that he says "some people" add is a small amount of "clay or scraped brick in memory of the clay." This would seem to be a rather extreme form of incorporating rather than inscribing memories. But as we shall see, although his is the first, it is by no means the last piece of evidence for the practice of putting ground or scraped potsherds into haroset in the quest for authenticity.

An additional recipe for haroset is found in the commentary on the Mishna by Rabbi Ovadiah ben Abraham Yareh MiBertinoro from northern Italy. Called "the Bartenura" after the name of his family's town of origin, Rabbi Ovadiah eventually left Italy to become leader of the religious Jewish community in Jerusalem at the end of the fifteenth century. His commentary on the Mishna has become the standard, much like Rashi's commentary on the Talmud.

---

31. Rashi calls haroset *aigros* in his commentary to an earlier talmudic discussion of haroset: Pesaḥim 40b. See chapter 3 for Rashi's haroset.
32. B. Laurioux, "Cuisines médiévales," in *Histoire de l'alimentation*, ed. J. L. Flandrin and M. Montanari (Paris: Fayard, 1996), 466.

In his recipe for haroset, the Bartenura mentions figs and apples, together with a larger variety of nuts than we have seen so far: hazelnuts and *botnim*, as well as almonds.[33] *Botnim* is the biblical term for pistachios (although in Modern Hebrew it is used for peanuts, which come from the New World, and would not have been available to him). He is presumably reporting a local custom, although pistachios and almonds appear together as early as the Book of Genesis, in the list of gifts sent by the patriarch Jacob to Pharaoh in Egypt, together with spices (Gen. 43:11). There they are called *zimrat haaretz,* the best fruits of the Land (of Israel). By including them in his haroset, the Bartenura evokes the memory of the patriarchs, incorporating yet another strand of Jewish history. Also interesting is his comment that haroset is present at the Seder not because it is a commandment, but because it is an antidote to the dangerous juices, or *kappa,* of the bitter herbs. This observation lends support to my suggestion in chapter 1 that haroset was introduced to the Seder table because of its supposed protective properties.

The Provençal and Italian recipes for haroset come from the border countries between Sepharad and Ashkenaz. They have unusual ingredients, some of them unique, like the *Shibbolei HaLeket*'s "blossoms from trees," but others shared by several recipes, such as the commonplace local chestnuts. They include a greater variety of nuts, like hazelnuts and pistachios. The spices, too, are more varied, including *teven mika,* cloves and nutmeg. With the addition of these ingredients, we begin to see the influence of local factors on the rabbinical tradition of haroset.

HAROSET IN MEDIEVAL ART

Up to now, all our information about haroset has come from written texts, from inscribed memories. But medieval Spain produced documentation of another sort. Under Moslem rule, the Jews enjoyed a Golden Age of literary and artistic production until the Christian conquest brought about their expulsion in 1492. Here in the Iberian peninsula it became customary to produce beautifully illustrated and illuminated texts of the Passover Haggada. While many of these illustrations focus on the

---

33. Rabbi Ovadiah ben Abraham Yareh MiBertinoro (c. 1450–before 1516), Commentary on Mishna Pesaḥim 10:3 *ad loc.*

biblical story of the Exodus from Egypt, some of them also commemorate in pictures contemporary ways of preparing for Passover, including making haroset.[34]

A late thirteenth- or fourteenth-century Haggada, illustrated in medieval Castille, and now in the British Library, contains a full-page illustration that shows two men pounding haroset in a large pot, using pestles almost as long as themselves, with a Hebrew caption that says, "They are making haroset."[35] From the way they are holding their pestles, one inside and one outside the pot, it looks as if they are taking turns pounding the haroset rhythmically (see picture insert, image 5).

The image clearly recalls the many texts, beginning with the Jerusalem Talmud, which discuss the crushing, grinding, or pounding of ingredients for haroset. It is also a visual reminder of why Yemenite haroset to this day is known as *dukkeh* ("pounded").

Spain was the leading, but not the only source for illustrated Haggadas. The Birds' Head Haggada, probably made in the German Rhineland at the beginning of the fourteenth century, contains a similar image of an oversized pestle used for making haroset.[36] Here the figure pounding the haroset, like the other figures in this Haggada, is drawn with a long-beaked bird's head. Perhaps the artist was concerned about transgressing the second of the Ten Commandments, which forbids graven images.[37] (For a picture, see insert, image 4.)

Returning to the Castillian Haggada, the illustration of pounding haroset is followed by an illustration of the distribution of haroset (see image 6).[38] Here a man stands over a large pot and ladles out haroset

---

34. Details of MSS come from T. Metzger and M. Metzger, *Jewish Life in the Middle Ages: Illuminated Hebrew Manuscripts of the Thirteenth to the Sixteenth Centuries* (New Jersey: Fine Art Books, 1982); M. Metzger, *La Haggada enluminée*, vol. 1 (Leiden: Brill, 1973). Dating and provenance follow: K. Kogman-Appel, *Illuminated Haggadot from Medieval Spain: Biblical Imagery and the Passover Holiday* (Pennsylvania: Pennsylvania University Press, 2006).

35. British Library Haggadah (Hispano-Moresque, Ms. Or. 2737, fol. 88 verso): Metzger (above, n. 34), 57 and pl. vii, fig. 26.

36. Jerusalem, Israel Museum: MS. 180/57.

37. It is of course impossible to know whether it was the artist or his patron who feared to transgress the commandment – if indeed this was the real reason for the birds' heads.

38. British Library Haggadah (MS. Or. 2737, fol. 89 recto), Metzger (above, n. 34), 58

into a small bowl held out to him by another man. A third figure is already turning his back to them and leaving with a bowl of haroset held high. The Hebrew caption, which says, "And he gives from them (*vezeh noten mihem*)," is not very clear. The correct Hebrew would say either "to them" or "of it."

Another Spanish Haggada, probably from fourteenth-century Aragon, known as the Sarajevo Haggada[39] – from the city where it first became known to modern scholarship – also illustrates the distribution of haroset.[40] The scene shows a seated figure ladling out haroset from a large pot into bowls proffered by other figures. Several people are leaving, having already filled their bowls. The Hebrew caption reads, "The master of the house gives haroset."

A third Iberian Haggada from around the same time, probably painted in Catalonia, and now housed in the British Library, also portrays the distribution of haroset.[41] A bearded and turbaned man in long robes is seated under an arch next to a pile of matzas, while in front of him a bearded servant in a tunic ladles out haroset. Three men in tunics stand waiting, with matzas in their hands.

Finally, an early fourteenth-century Haggada from Barcelona shows the distribution of haroset, this time in the form of balls.[42] The picture, one of four on the page, shows very fine detail against a gold background. A richly bearded and turbaned man in long robes sits under a canopy or an arch, with an empty bag at his feet. He is gesturing to his three servants, dressed only in tunics. Behind him, a servant transfers

and pl. vii, fig. 28.

39. It has also been suggested that the Sarajevo Haggada might have been illustrated in Castille or Provence.

40. Sarajevo Haggada, fol. 33 verso, in the National Museum of Bosnia and Herzegovina in Sarajevo. Information about the Haggada is taken from C. Roth, ed., *The Sarajevo Haggadah* (Beograd: Izdavacki Zavod, 1963); see also Metzger (above, n. 34), 59–60, pl. vii, fig. 26. Metzger and Metzger (above, n. 34) write that it is Sephardic, probably from Aragon, c. 1350–60.

41. London, British Library: MS. Or. 2884, fol. 17 recto. Metzger (above, n. 34), 61, pl. vi, fig. 25.

42. London, British Library: Golden Haggadah, MS. Add. 27210, fol. 15 recto (upper register left). Metzger (above, n. 34), 60–1; Metzger and Metzger (above, n. 34), pl. 318 (color); Kogman-Appel (above, n. 34), color pl. 2.

balls of haroset from a large pot to a smaller dish, which another servant hands to a group of children with outstretched arms and to a sad but pretty mother with her swaddled baby. Another servant distributes matzas from a basket. The Hebrew caption says, "The master of the house gives orders to give matzas and haroset to the children" (see picture insert, image 7).

Although I could find no written record for the custom, I did come across some modern oral traditions of serving a ball of haroset to each person at the Seder. They all came from women of Sephardic or Mizrahi origin. Val Mars, who comes from the Sephardic Montefiore family, gave me a recipe for haroset in the form of balls, as did Linette Cohen from the priestly Jewish community of Jerba in Tunisia, and Dina Lavi from Tripoli in Libya. Thus these women are transmitting a tradition that dates back to the Middle Ages. Their recipes appear in the final chapter of this book.

The distribution of haroset depicted in these Haggadas clearly did not take place at the Seder; most of the figures are standing, not sitting or reclining. It has been customary, since the nineteenth century at least, to distribute money to the poor so that they would be able to buy *kimḥa dePisḥa,* flour for Passover, for baking matzas.[43] The ingredients of the haroset were much more expensive than flour, though a much smaller quantity was needed. Most expensive of all were the spices imported from the East. Economic historians have calculated the cost of spices in the Middle Ages compared with other foodstuffs. In Antwerp in the 1430s, for example, a skilled craftsman would earn eight pence a day. For a penny, he could buy a gallon of milk or a pint of butter. A pound of ginger, however, would cost almost two whole days' wages, a pound of cinnamon three days' wages, while a pound of cloves would cost four and a half days' wages. In fourteenth-century Barcelona, different grades of ginger ranged from four to ten pence a pound, while cloves, imported from the distant Molucca islands, were about fifteen times this price.[44]

---

43. To this day the charity collected in synagogues before Passover is called *kimḥa dePisḥa;* it is used for buying matza and other Passover needs.

44. J. Munro, "Oriental Spices and Their Costs in Medieval Cuisine: Luxuries or Necessities?": lecture given at the University of Toronto, 1988, posted at https://www.economics.utoronto.ca/munro5/SPICES1.htm (accessed April 2018); Freedman (above, n. 23), 126–8.

It would seem likely, then, that some communities undertook a distribution of haroset with its very expensive spices before Passover, so that everyone could celebrate the Seder at home. Such community distributions of haroset are in fact recorded in nineteenth-century Iraqi communities, and the popular etymology of the Iraqi name for haroset, *ḥallek* (which we saw used by the *Geonim*), attributes it to the Hebrew word for distribution, *ḥaluka*. Though hundreds of years separate the Haggada illuminations from the recorded practice, I would like to suggest that they record some form of distribution of haroset to the poor before Passover, by the community or by rich individuals. The recipe from Lunel, above, with its enormous quantities, might reflect this practice.

HAROSET IN MEDIEVAL VERSE

Apart from the scholarly and rabbinic works we have seen so far, medieval Provence provided a new literary source for haroset traditions, also written by rabbis: satirical poetry. Talmudic literature included lighter moments, or even jokes, but there was no sustained literary satire as such. In thirteenth- or fourteenth-century Arles in Provence, Kalonymos ben Kalonymos (also known as Maestro Calo) wrote a long satirical poem called *Even Boḥan* (The Touchstone), in which he looks briefly at all the festivals in turn, satirizing their customs in general, and the process of haroset making in particular.[45] Kalonymos' poetry is full of talmudic and scriptural allusions. Here is a section on Passover, describing the preparations for the festival:

> On the fourteenth [of Nisan] at dusk
> The time when we left Egypt
> Israelite lads in opposing ranks
> Grind with mills or pound in mortars (*dakhu bamedokhah*)
> To make haroset from a collection of different kinds
> In memory of the mud (*teet*) of Raamses and the clay and the bricks.
> Each of them expects and looks forward

---

45. Kalonymos ben Kalonymos, *Even Boḥan*, ed. A. M. Habermann (Tel Aviv: Maḥberot LaSifrut, 1956). My translation.

> To the time when they will finish making it acidic and thick
> They will strew on it "all the chief spices" (*besamim rosh*) so that
> it will be ready
> And buy their spice from the spice merchants
> And after this, when they have rested and revived
> The people will go out and gather
> From gardens far and near
> Herbs and vegetables
> One will ask for the lettuce and will look for endives
> Another will pursue *karpas*
> Another will desire perfect greens
> And another will seek *amrirata*
> And if there is none, will fall back on the ruling of Ravina
> And use just *tamkha* and *ḥarḥavina* [as bitter herbs].

It is doubtful, of course, how far we can rely on satirical works for evidence of what really happened. The problem is compounded by the fact that rabbis writing about Passover often relied on earlier texts, rather than recording the customs of their own time. We can clearly identify some of Kalonymos' vignettes in talmudic literature. For example, the reference to buying spices from the merchants takes us right back to R. Elazar b. Tzadok; Kalonymos uses the same talmudic vocabulary. But some new images here may well reflect how people prepared for Passover in Kalonymos' medieval Provence. Kalonymos clearly enjoys his satirical metaphor of the lads making haroset lined up as if for battle.[46] Haroset here is made by a group of lads, who take on the hard work of grinding and pounding, perhaps doing it together for the entire community. The poem may even refer to rhythmic pounding by turns, a practice suggested by the illustration, noted earlier, in the British Library's Haggada from Castille.[47] In contrast, the people seek their bitter herbs individually, with each choosing one of the several sorts listed by the Mishna.

---

46. Perhaps we can recognize here the sort of Jews, still familiar to us today, who prepare for their Passover as if conducting a military campaign.

47. MS. Or. 2737, fol. 88 verso. Metzger (above, n. 34), 57 and pl. vii, fig. 26.

Kalonymos' spices also appear to reflect the local traditions of his contemporary Provence. The poet notes the use of "all the chief spices" (*besamim rosh*), introduced by the Provençal *Baalei HaAsufot*. Similarly, the practice of strewing spices on the haroset, rather than incorporating them, was mentioned by Rabbi Ovadiah of Bertinoro in the fifteenth century.

The Passover section of *Even Bohan* ends with a satirical piece directed against women. The master of the house, addressing his wife, uses the vocabulary of the erotic Song of Songs, as well as a misogynist passage from the Book of Esther (among other allusions). He is pacifying her for all the hard work she has put into preparing for Passover, implying that she is compensated with very expensive clothes, as well as by eating the festive meat she has prepared:

> The master of the house when his heart is merry at his feast (Est. 1:10)
> Will pile consolations on his revered rib (Gen. 1:18; 22)[48]
> Saying: "You, the mistress of the house
> How you have toiled today! My soul pains me (Is. 15:4)
> When I see how much you sighed and cried (Ezek. 9:4)![49]
> And now, my sister (Song. 4:9–12)[50]
> Be happy and rejoice (Zech. 2:12) and celebrate your festival
> Arise and eat your fill of meat
> Hurry and wear the garments of your glory (Is. 52:1)
> [Which cost?] ten thousand gold drachmas."

He ends, however, in all seriousness, with two lines of the Hallel, the verses of praise that are recited at the Seder: "This is the day which the Lord hath made; we will rejoice and be glad in it" (Ps. 118:27). This quotation comes from the festival liturgy. We will come across this combination of the serious and the playful when we reach the early modern period, and discuss in chapter 4 the word games people played with haroset.

---

48. This is, of course, an allusion to Eve, made out of Adam's rib to be a "help meet for him."
49. The satirical reference here is to the wicked who "sigh and cry" for abominations.
50. "My sister, my spouse."

Chapter 3

Haroset Moves North: Medieval Ashkenaz

"And there are of course *other* kinds, made from other ingredients. But this is the way we make it in our family."

She saw the little girl give each ingredient a look to rehearse it in her mind. As if she were bowing slightly to each, in its turn.

"Apples and raisins. Walnuts. Honey. Wine ..."

..."*Roshinkes mit mandelen*," the grandmother said.

David Mamet, *Passover*

The quotation above defines David Mamet's modern Ashkenazic haroset. His use of Yiddish, the language of Ashkenaz, for the *rozhinkes mit mandelen*, raisins with almonds, underlines the cultural context. The development of the Ashkenazic traditions of haroset was complex. It is a long story, and I will trace how the ingredients in haroset, and their symbolism, changed over time. I will explore how the traditions were passed on from grandmother to granddaughter, from father to son, from master to pupil, from community to community. Medieval Ashkenaz was home to the rabbinic authorities who first expanded the range of ingredients of haroset, inspired by the fruits and spices in the Song of Songs. Paradoxically, Ashkenazic haroset today is almost always the same everywhere, while it is the Sephardim who have many, many variations. As we shall see, this was not always the case.

THE BEGINNINGS OF THE ASHKENAZIC
TRADITION: RASHI AND THE TOSAFISTS

In the search through the books written by Ashkenazic rabbis, I begin with Rashi. This is where Jewish children have traditionally begun their Torah studies for many hundreds of years. Rashi (whose name is an acronym for Rabbi Solomon ben Isaac) was born in Troyes in Champagne in northern France in the year 1040. He lived through troubled times. The end of his life was marred by the massacres of the First Crusade, when thousands of French Jews, including many of Rashi's own friends and relatives, were killed.

Rashi wrote many books, including a commentary on most of the Babylonian Talmud, which appears in the margins of every standard printed edition to this day, in a special cursive Hebrew typeface which is now identified with his works.[1] Rashi's main discussion of haroset appears in the Babylonian Talmud, beginning with the statement of R. Levi that haroset is in memory of the apple:[2]

> *In memory of the apple*: Because they [the Jewish women in Egypt] used to give birth to their children there without pain, so that the Egyptians would not know about them, as it says: "I roused thee under the apple tree" (Song. 8:5). *Make it thick*: Take it and crush it a great deal so that it will be thick. You must make it acidic, putting apples in it and wine, whatever makes it acidic. *You must make it acidic*: In memory of the apple and you must make

---

1. This typeface, although identified with Rashi and commonly used for printing his works, in fact postdates him by hundreds of years.
2. It is unclear whether Rashi himself really wrote the commentary on this particular chapter of Pesaḥim, or whether it is only attributed to him.

it thick in memory of the clay. *Spice*: greens (*yerakot*) which you put in the haroset in memory of the straw, which you crush into it finely in memory of the clay.[3]

Thus Rashi, in eleventh-century Ashkenaz, included in his haroset sour apples crushed to a thick paste, wine and green herbs or vegetables (*yerakot*). Incidentally, Rashi is the first authority I have found to list wine rather than vinegar. He lived in Champagne, famed for its vineyards (although the sparkling wine we call champagne had not yet been invented), and like many of the local Jews, himself played a considerable part in the wine trade.[4] Perhaps wine, then, was easier or cheaper to obtain than vinegar. Rashi explains that the purpose of the wine (and the apples) is to make haroset acidic, so clearly he intends a dry or sour wine. In his commentary earlier in Pesahim, he translates haroset as *aigros*, sour (as in the French for vinegar, *vin aigre*, sour wine), and describes it as a strong condiment which included vinegar, used as a sauce for meat.[5]

The word *yerakot*, used by Rashi to explain the spices, means literally "greens," and may refer to herbs or any vegetable, green or otherwise. Since they come here under the heading of "spices" and are in memory of the straw, it is tempting to translate these greens as "herbs." We have seen that the herbs thyme and hyssop were added to Maimonides' Sephardic version of haroset. Sadly, we do not know what herbs Rashi used, but we shall see below that about a hundred years later, the *Roke'ah* added *karpas*, the green leaves used for the first dipping at the Seder table, to the haroset. This can be any green leafy vegetable; nowadays it is usually parsley or celery.

Interestingly, a sour green sauce, *sauce verte*, made with ground parsley or sorrel or sage, combined with ginger and vinegar (or *verjuice*, made of sour unripe grapes) was very popular as a sauce for meat and fish in medieval France. It appears more than once in the fourteenth-century

---

3. Pesahim 116a.
4. H. Soloveitchik, *Principles and Pressures: Jewish Trade in Gentile Wine in the Middle Ages* (Tel Aviv: Am Oved, 2003 [Hebrew]), 91–2. Sparkling champagne wine as we know it was first produced by Dom Perignon in the late seventeenth century.
5. Pesahim 40b.

cookbook, the *Viandier de Taillevent*.[6] This sauce was also commonly hawked around the streets of medieval Paris.[7] It was usually made with breadcrumbs, which could not have been used on Passover. If Rashi's sauce was based on *sauce verte*, he must have used something else to thicken it.

I was surprised and delighted to read in Joan Nathan's book on the cuisine of present-day French Jewry, which we have already encountered in chapter 2, that some contemporary French Jews have a custom of using *sauce verte* at their Passover meal, although apparently not as haroset.[8] Joan suggested that broken matza or matza meal can be substituted for the breadcrumbs.

Rashi's grandson, Rabbi Samuel ben Meir, or the Rashbam, also wrote a commentary on the Babylonian Talmud. On our passage from Pesaḥim, he writes that you put the *yerakot* in the haroset to make it thick. We saw above that Rashi mentioned *yerakot* in the context of spices that recall the straw, and I suggested that they refer to herbs. Here, however, the *yerakot* are meant to affect the texture, not the taste of the haroset, so it is more likely that Rashbam is referring to vegetables in general, and not to spicy herbs. Perhaps these were less expensive than other ingredients and could be used to provide bulk. I will show yet another possibility below in the Ravan's haroset.

I noted that every page of the standard editions of the Babylonian Talmud has an additional column of commentary by Rashi at the side of the page. In dialogue with Rashi, at the other side of the same page, are the comments of the Tosafists, his successors as commentators on the Babylonian Talmud. Among the first were Rabbenu Tam, another grandson, and his pupils. The Tosafists' commentaries are *tosafot*, literally "additions," and they continue until the fourteenth century.

---

6. J. Prescott, trans., *Viandier de Taillevent* (Bibliothèque Nationale MS), no. 215: green sauce (*sauce verte*), http://www.telusplanet.net/public/prescotj/data/viandier/viandier5.html (accessed April 2018).

7. T. Scully, *The Art of Cookery in the Middle Ages* (Woodbridge: Boydell Press, 1995; repr. 2002), 13–4.

8. J. Nathan, *Quiches, Kugel and Couscous: My Search for Jewish Cooking in France* (New York: Knopf, 2010). I am grateful to Joan Nathan for discussion of *sauce verte*.

On our passage in Pesaḥim 116a, the Tosafists write:

> *You must make [the haroset] thick and you must make it acidic.* In the Jerusalem Talmud it says it should be made in memory of the blood, which is why it is called dipping – into a liquid. And with it [you need] something to make it thick, and at the time of eating you dilute it with wine and vinegar. The *Teshuvot HaGeonim* explains that you should make haroset from fruits that the community of Israel is compared to in the Song of Songs: "I roused thee under the apple tree" (8:5); "like a piece of a pomegranate"(4:3); "the fig tree puts forth her green figs" (2:13); "I said, 'I will go up into the palm tree'" (7:8); ..."I went down into the garden of nuts" (6:11).

The reference to the Jerusalem Talmud is particularly interesting. The Babylonian Talmud is recognized as the authoritative basis for Jewish law to this day, and rabbinical commentators rarely cite the Jerusalem Talmud. Here, however, the Tosafists relate to the controversy between those who wanted their haroset thick like clay, or more runny, like blood. They propose mixing in wine or vinegar at the time of eating. All previous sources had proposed kneading in the vinegar earlier, to keep the mixture thick like clay. We will see that some later Tosafists explained the addition of liquids prior to eating as a solution to the question of whether haroset should be thick or runny: made thick at first, the haroset was then thinned down at table with wine or vinegar.

The Tosafists introduced an innovation that proved very important in the development of haroset. Quoting the *Teshuvot HaGeonim*, they write that haroset should be made from fruits to which the Jewish people are compared in the Song of Songs: apples, pomegranates, figs, dates and nuts. Up till now, several rabbis had cited R. Levi's quotation from the Babylonian Talmud about the apple from the Song of Songs. Rashi was the first to allude to the midrash on this verse. Rabbi David, the grandson of Maimonides, added nuts. So now, we have an authority for widening the whole range of ingredients: if one ingredient from the Song of Songs is recommended, why not the rest? But the Tosafists are not satisfied with fruit that is merely *mentioned* in the Song of

Songs. They are interested, specifically, in fruits which are *allegorized* in the midrashim on the Song of Songs as metaphors for the Jewish people.

The Tosafists also add almonds: "And almonds (*shekedim*) because God watches over (*shoked*) the End [of Days]." This explanation probably refers to a passage in Jeremiah 1:11–12:

> "Moreover the word of the Lord came to me, saying,
> 'What doest thou see, Jeremiah?'
> And I said, 'I see a rod of an almond tree (*shaked*).'
> Then the Lord said to me,
> 'Thou hast seen well,
> For I am watchful (*shoked*) to bring my word to pass.'"[9]

Though they do not appear in the Song of Songs, the almonds allude to the final redemption. They sweeten the haroset metaphorically, as well as materially.

In this way, more symbolic foods were added to the Seder table, some of which would pave the way toward sweeter haroset in general. Nonetheless, it is ironic that it was the Ashkenazic Tosafists, relying on the *Teshuvot HaGeonim*, who widened the possibilities for ingredients in the haroset, as Ashekenazic haroset today has the least variation in ingredients.

In taking care to identify every ingredient in the haroset with the Jewish people, the Tosafists were creating prospective memories. By eating haroset, every Jew was incorporating the memories and myths of the past, identifying him- or herself in the present, and alluding to the redemption which was and the redemption yet to come.

HAROSET ACROSS THE CHANNEL: PRE-EXPULSION ENGLAND

All of England's Jews were expelled in 1290, and we have limited documentation about the medieval community. Fortunately, two commentaries on the Passover Haggada, written not long before the expulsion, survived.

---

9. *Jerusalem Bible*: "For I will hasten my word to perform it."

In the first, Rabbi Moses Elijah of London (also known as the Ram MiLondres)[10] talks about using all the fruits mentioned in the Song of Songs – dates, figs, pomegranates, nuts and apples – in haroset. Like his contemporary Continental Tosafists, he takes this list from the various fruits described in the Song of Songs. His spices, *sanbal* (spikenard) and cinnamon, also come from the Song of Songs.[11] Thus, Rabbi Elijah's early English haroset is similar to that of his European contemporaries. Like them, he stresses its acidity, and adds almonds to the fruit of the Songs of Songs as another example of God's care for His people.

Rabbi Elijah's pupil, Rabbi Jacob ben Judah Hazan MiLondres, wrote a book of laws and customs called the *Etz Ḥayim* (The Tree of Life) in London, in 1287.[12] Rabbi Jacob begins his recipe for haroset using the words of Maimonides, who in his later recipe wrote that haroset was a mitzva, a religious obligation "according to the scribes." Like Maimonides, he specifies dates, dried figs and raisins, and says that they are to be "trodden," before adding vinegar and spices.[13] It is interesting to see how the influence of the *Mishneh Torah*, written in Egypt at the beginning of the twelfth century, was already so widespread that it was cited as an authority for haroset by an Ashkenazic rabbi in London before the end of the century.

Rabbi Jacob then quotes a more immediate authority, Rabbi Elijah, citing his predecessor's views on the fruit from the Song of Songs. Rabbi Jacob continues to quote him with the reference to the Jerusalem Talmud and explains that the haroset is made thick at first, but at the Seder table, just before dipping the bitter herbs into it, it is

---

10. M. Y. L. Sacks with C. Roth, eds., *The Writings of Rabbi Elijah of London* (Jerusalem: Mosad HaRav Kook, 1956 [Hebrew, with preface in English]), 153.

11. Arabic terms such as *sanbal* are described by Rabbi Elijah as *laaz*, the vernacular. Since Arabic was hardly the spoken language in medieval London, we can see from this how closely he was following his rabbinic sources (perhaps Maimonides in this case: see Rabbi Jacob below) even when he did not understand what was meant. The use of these unfamiliar words led to problems for his copyists and clearly increased the number of corruptions in the MS.

12. Rabbi Jacob ben Judah Hazan MiLondres, *Etz Ḥayim*, ed. I. Brodie (Jerusalem: Mosad HaRav Kook, 1962–67).

13. The text has "spice them with spice like clay with spice." This is probably a scribal error: the last *tavlin*, spice, should be corrected to *teven*, straw.

made runny by the addition of liquid, so that it resembles both clay *and* blood. In the Babylonian Talmud, Abbaye had reconciled the two opinions that haroset should be both thick and acidic; Rabbi Elijah, as quoted by his pupil Rabbi Jacob, manages to reconcile two opposing opinions as well.

With the direct quotation from Maimonides, these English versions of haroset give the impression of being text-based traditions, rather than practical instructions. We may wonder whether any Jews really managed to get hold of pomegranates in thirteenth-century England, or whether, like some of their European contemporaries, they simply used apples and nuts for their haroset. In 1289, "fifteen lemons, seven oranges and two hundred and thirty pomegranates" were bought from a Spanish ship at Portsmouth for Eleanor of Castille, the queen of England, homesick for the fruit of her native Spain.[14] However, a treasured fruit acquired as a rare exception for the queen herself is rather unlikely to have been regularly available for her Jewish subjects every Passover. This said, it is possible that Jews on the continent of Europe at least may have had access to dried rather than fresh pomegranates.[15] *Le Ménagier de Paris*, a Parisian book of housekeeping from the late fourteenth century, records that products available at an *especier*, a spice seller, included not only spices, but also various exotic foods such as dried pomegranates and candied nuts and sweets.[16]

ASHKENAZ IN SEPHARAD: THE ROSH AND THE *TUR*

Rabbi Asher ben Yehiel, called Asheri or the Rosh, lived in Troyes and Worms, and was the leader of the German Jewish community. After he fled to Spain in 1303, he became the spiritual head of the Spanish Jewish community, dying in Toledo. Thus the Rosh moved from Ashkenaz to Sepharad, but still kept to the traditions of Ashkenaz. His major work was a commentary on the Babylonian Talmud. He wrote little about

---

14. S. Paston-Williams, *The Art of Dining: A History of Cooking and Eating* (London: National Trust, 1995), 35.

15. See P. Freedman, *Out of the East: Spices and the Medieval Imagination* (New Haven/ London: Yale University Press, 2008), 48.

16. A translation of the *Ménagier* may be found at http://www.daviddfriedman.com/ Medieval/Cookbooks/Menagier/Menagier.html (accessed April 2018).

haroset, other than to quote from the Babylonian Talmud and then add the briefest of details, saying that the spices should be like cinnamon and *sonbal* (spikenard), which are like straw.

The Rosh's son, Rabbi Jacob ben Asher, fled with him. Unlike his father, whose commentary followed the text of the Talmud, Rabbi Jacob codified all of Jewish law in his four-part book, *Arbaa HaTurim* (The Four Rows or Columns), subdivided by topic and section. He is thus also known as the *Baal HaTurim* (the Master of the *Turim*), or simply, the *Tur*. His work proved highly influential and set the pattern for later codes of Jewish law.

In dealing with the laws of Passover, the *Tur* attributes to Rabbi Yehiel the reconciliation of the two differing opinions in the Jerusalem Talmud that haroset should be thick like clay and runny like blood.[17] Following the *Etz Ḥayim* of London, he taught that the haroset, initially made thick, should be thinned down with vinegar at the Seder table.[18] His haroset, made of apples, nuts, figs, cinnamon and ginger, and thinned down with vinegar, is firmly in the tradition of the Ashkenazic scholars we have encountered. However, like the author of the Provençal *Sefer Baalei HaAsufot*, the *Tur* tells us that his haroset is in memory of clay, and also of the bitter herbs. He believed, though, that the bitter herbs should be represented by the sour or acidic taste of apples, unlike the *Sefer Baalei HaAsufot* which required a bitter ingredient, and unlike his other predecessors for whom the sourness was in memory of the apple.

Up to now it has been only the scholars of Ashkenaz who have quoted the Jerusalem Talmud's instruction that haroset should be thick like clay and thin like blood, together with the compromise of Rabbi Elijah of London and Rabbi Yehiel, that it should be made thick at first and then thinned down with wine or vinegar at table. Now we see how this instruction arrived in Sepharad with the *Tur*, who moved to Spain. Indeed, the only families I have been able to find who thin their haroset

---

17. Rabbi Yehiel may have been Rabbi Yehiel of Paris, a French Tosafist who was involved in the disputations with Christians which ended in the burning of the Talmud in the 1240s.
18. *Tur, Oraḥ Ḥayim, Hilkhot Pesaḥ* 473.

with wine at the Seder today are of Sephardic descent: the Vaturi family from Tripoli in Libya, Eli Zanou from the Bnei Zion community in Algeria, the Dahan family from Teheran and the Benadys from Gibraltar (who add vinegar rather than wine). None of my modern informants, however, knew that this practice was in memory of blood.

We should note a further intriguing detail. Unlike his father, who stipulated cinnamon and *sonbal* (spikenard) for haroset, the *Tur* specified cinnamon and *ginger*. This difference probably did not reflect changing taste preferences or availability, as both spikenard and ginger were common in Europe of the Middle Ages.[19] But *sonbal* written in Hebrew letters is very similar to *zangvil*, the word used by his father, the Rosh, for ginger. It looks as if here too we may have a change in tradition caused by a scribal error. Having reached this conclusion myself from reading the texts, I found I had been preempted several hundred years ago by Rabbi Joseph ben David, who had pointed out this possibility in his *Beit David* (House of David), published in 1740.[20]

ASHKENAZ IN THE FIFTEENTH CENTURY

Moving north again to fifteenth-century Ashkenaz, the next treatment of haroset comes from the Maharil, Rabbi Jacob ben Moses Mollin from Mainz in Germany (1360–1427), who wrote *Sefer HaMinhagim*, the Book of Customs.[21] In it, he specifies that *kida* and cinnamon should be added to haroset in the form of long strips, like straw. *Kida* or *ketzia* (*ketziata* in Aramaic) seems to refer to cassia, a spice made of tree bark, like cinnamon. It appears as an ingredient of the incense in the Tabernacle (Ex. 30:24) and, later, in the Temple, according to the rabbis of the Talmud.[22] The Maharil also quotes some opinions that pomegranate should be added to haroset to make it sour. One wonders if he ever tasted pomegranates, which are sweet-sour rather than sour.

---

19. Cf. B. Laurioux, "Spices in the Medieval Diet: A New Approach," *Food and Foodways* 1 (1985): 43–76.
20. Rabbi Joseph ben David, *Beit David* (Salonica: Betzalel Ashkenazi Press, 1740), sect. 79, 254.
21. Jacob Mollin, *Sefer Maharil: Minhagim*, ed. S. Spitzer (Jerusalem: Makhon Yerushalayim, 1989).
22. Y. Yoma 41a; Keritot 6a.

The Maharil is one of the few scholars to discuss where to put the haroset, *maror* and *karpas*. He notes opinions that these Seder foods should be put in dishes separate from the matza, so that when the matza is removed from the table they will still be in sight of the children who will ask the Four Questions. The Maharil's is the first reference I have found to the six little dishes we use today for the foods on the Seder plate.

Another fifteenth-century German work, *Leket Yosher* (The Collection of Righteousness), relates at length to haroset.[23] It was written by Rabbi Joseph (Joselein) ben Moses, from Hochstadt in Bavaria, who quoted as his authority his teacher, Rabbi Israel ben Petahya Isserlein from Vienna, the author of *Terumot HaDeshen* (Sweeping the Ashes).[24]

The *Leket Yosher* also includes further details of ingredients. He knows and cites the view that haroset should be made from the fruits to which Israel is compared in the Song of Songs and elsewhere. He also includes pears. Interestingly, he is not the first authority to do so. Rabbi Samuel ben Solomon (the Rash) from Falaise in Normandy, a Tosafist of the twelfth to thirteenth centuries, wrote a commentary on an anonymous poem that is sometimes added to the synagogue service for *Shabbat HaGadol*, the Sabbath before Passover.[25] This poem, *El Elohei HaRuhot LeKhol Basar* (God, the God of the Spirits of all Flesh), lists the laws of Passover. Rabbi Samuel's commentary is appended to a better-known book of halakhot, the *Or Zarua* (Light is Sown) written by Rabbi Isaac ben Moses of Vienna.

Rabbi Samuel does not describe how haroset is made, but he alludes to the process with an interesting attempt to explain the word "*haroset*." He cites the commentary of Rashi on a verse in Jeremiah (19:2), which mentions the *Harsit* Gate. Rashi quotes the *Targum*, the Aramaic translation of the Bible, which translates *Harsit* Gate as the Dung Gate

---

23. *Leket Yosher* 73.
24. Rabbi Joseph ben Moses, *Leket Yosher*, "Including *Minhagim*, Halakhic Rulings and Responsa of the *Gaon*, his Rabbi [Israel ben Petahya Isserlein], Author of *Terumot HaDeshen*," ed. J. Freimann (Berlin: Itzkowski, 1903; repr. Jerusalem: no publisher, 1964). "Sweeping the ashes" refers to the work of the priests at the altar in the Tabernacle and Temple (e.g. Lev. 6:10–11).
25. Rabbi Samuel also wrote the famous mnemonic rhyme for the order of the Seder (*Kadesh URehatz*), sung before the Seder begins.

in Jerusalem. The word "*ḥaroset*," which is similar to "*ḥarsit*," must thus mean things mixed and crushed like refuse.

Like Rashi, Rabbi Samuel included *yerakot*, greens, in his haroset, and like him says it should be acidic in memory of the apple and thick in memory of the clay.[26] But then, for what appears to be the first time in history, he mentions pears as an ingredient, together with apples and nuts. He does not explain this. The other fruits mentioned are associated with biblical verses, but pears do not appear in the Bible. They are mentioned only rarely in the Mishna and Jerusalem Talmud, and not once in the Babylonian Talmud.

Rabbi Samuel is, in fact, somewhat perplexing. He mentions the midrash about the apple tree and then continues, "Therefore put in apples, pears and nuts because Israel was compared with the nut." Thus apples and nuts are explained, but not pears. There is no other evidence of the use of pears at this stage (and they do not appear again for two hundred years until the time of the *Leket Yosher*). Morever, this text is rather confused and misspelt, and we might have suspected a mistake by a later copyist, who presumed an ingredient he was accustomed to, but which might not necessarily have been in the original text. However, a recent edition of Rabbi Samuel's commentary shows that pears are present in all the manuscripts. The editor even notes that this is their first appearance as an ingredient of haroset.[27]

Returning now to the *Leket Yosher*, it is clear that by the fifteenth century, the inhabitants of northern Ashkenaz were accustomed to using pears in their haroset:

> And he [the Mahariv[28]] explained that it is a mitzva to put pomegranates and all the fruits mentioned in the Song of Songs in haroset, but he does not know why pears (*biren*) should be put in haroset, but anyway one should not change this *minhag*

---

26. Rabbi Isaac ben Moses of Vienna, *Or Zarua*, ed. A. Marienberg (Jerusalem: Or Etzion Institute for Torah, 2006), 2, 119b.

27. *Or Zarua*, ed. Marienberg.

28. The Mahariv was Rabbi Jacob ben Judah Weil, a fifteenth-century Ashkenazi halakhic authority, who is often cited together with the *Terumot HaDeshen*.

(custom). I also remember that I heard from my father Rabbi Moses that one should put pears in haroset in the same amount as apples and nuts so that it should be the same color as clay (*teet*), but generally the *Gaon* says it should be made thick like clay. However, we have not seen in the literature that it should be made the same color as clay.[29]

The *Leket Yosher* also notes that pears "are common here," and although he can find no reason for this popular custom, he does not object to it. Once a local tradition has been established, there appears to be a reluctance to change it, even if there is no mention of it in the rabbinical texts. Presumably the use of pears was for practical reasons. They were common and readily available locally from winter storage and, as the *Leket Yosher* explains, they gave the haroset the desired consistency and color, as pears turn brick red when exposed to the air.

Indeed, pears are clearly evident in the illustrations and captions of fifteenth-century German illuminated Haggadas. The Haggada now known as the Yahudah Haggada[30] shows a man in a hat using pestle and mortar (with a lip for pouring) next to a table, where another man with a liripipe, a medieval headdress with a long tail, is peeling fruit with a large knife. There are two bowls of fruit on the table. The illustration is captioned with a rhyming Hebrew couplet: "Haroset in memory of the clay they prepare/[From] nuts, apples and pear." (See this image in the picture insert, image 8.)

Pears appear in another German Haggada known to modern scholars as the Second Nuremberg Haggada.[31] Here, again, we have a caption in Hebrew verse: "The two brothers the haroset prepare/From nuts, apples and pear." In the Nuremberg Haggada, we can even see some yellow-brown pears in a basket on the table. The illustration in this

---

29. *Leket Yosher* (above, n. 24), part 1 (*Oraḥ Ḥayim*), 83, sect. 5.
30. Israel Museum, MS. 180/50. The illustrations were painted around 1460–70.
31. The Second Nuremberg Haggada, now in the collection of David Sofer, used to be called Schocken MS. 24087. A reproduction is now available on-line at http://jnul.huji.ac.il/dl/mss-pr/mss_d_0076/index.html (accessed March 2013). It was painted c. 1460–70. I am grateful to David Sofer for permission to reproduce this illustration.

Haggada is very similar to that of the Yahudah Haggada, even down to the shape of the mortar.[32] (See this image in the picture insert, image 9.)

Another confirmation of pears in haroset comes from an unexpected source. Antonio Margaritha was the son of an early sixteenth-century German rabbi who converted to Christianity. He was the author of *Der Ganz Jüdisch Glaub* (The Whole Jewish Religion), a hostile account of Judaism. In spite of his hostility, he does include some accurate details. He describes the customs of the Seder, mentioning a mixture made of *öpfel, piren, unnd nussenn* (apples, pears and nuts) mixed with wine and strewn with very good spices.[33] This is clearly haroset, although he does not mention it by name. He also notes that the initial letters of the ingredients spell the word *ev"en* (=öp"n), "stone" in Hebrew. He adds that the Jews explain that this mixture is made into the shape of a brick in memory of the bricks made in Egypt by their forefathers.

But the addition of pears is an exception. In general, after the early medieval Tosafists had *expanded* the possibilities for different ingredients in haroset by recommending the fruits and spices of the Song of Songs, the later rabbis of Ashkenaz were beginning to *restrict* them. In the *Leket Yosher*, we find rabbinical restrictions on several ingredients. *Sefer Ravia*, in the twelfth century, had listed sour apples and nuts as the main ingredients of haroset, in what was becoming the standard Ashkenazic version. All the authorities agreed on these, but there is the first sign that this was not the case with figs. *Ravia*, alluding to the verse in the Song of Songs (2:13) that says, "The fig tree puts forth her green figs" (Song. 2:13), writes that "there are those who put in figs." This careful wording seems to imply that there were some rabbis who did *not* use figs, for figs presented a problem. Dried figs commonly develop a whitish, powdery coating, composed of sugar crystals, which result from the drying process. This white powder was often mistakenly identified as flour, and some rabbis were concerned that it might come into contact

---

32. On these Haggadas and the relationship between them, see K. Kogman-Appel, *Die zweite Nürnberger und die Jehuda Haggada: Jüdische Illustratoren zwischen Tradition und Fortschritt* (Frankfurt am Main: P. Lang, 1998).

33. A. Margaritha, *Der Ganz Jüdisch Glaub* (Augspurg: no publisher, 1530), 27.

with water, ferment and become leaven, which is forbidden on Passover.[34] Ravia thus takes pains to point out that the white powder usually found on dried figs is not flour.

However, by the fifteenth century the *Leket Yosher* bans dried figs, and even the bay leaves (*Lorberblatte*) packed with the figs. He also applies his ban to dried grapes and shelled almonds, although almonds protected by their shells were not in danger of contamination by leaven and could be used in haroset.

The *Leket Yosher* also discusses the process of using haroset at the Seder itself. He was particularly concerned with the case of Passover which coincides with the Sabbath, when various cooking processes permitted on a weekday are forbidden.[35] This situation would have presented a problem for scholars who resolved the Jerusalem Talmud disagreement over the nature of haroset by making it thick, and then thinning it with wine or vinegar immediately before eating it at the Seder. Adding liquid to the haroset could be considered "kneading" (as when water is added to flour), and thus forbidden on the Sabbath. The *Leket Yosher* here reported that he saw his rabbi, the author of *Terumot HaDeshen*, solve this dilemma by using his finger to mix the wine into the haroset, performing this action in a different way from usual, so that it would not be considered "kneading."

The path toward our modern Ashkenazic haroset was being prepared. But, as we have seen, these rulings did not appear to affect the Sephardic communities, nor the communities of the border countries, of Provence and Italy.

BITTER HERBS IN HAROSET

Up to now, we have encountered haroset which was sweet, sour and a mixture of sweet and sour together. However, there appears to have been a tradition of including sharp or bitter tastes in the haroset as well. Its origin can be traced to the border lands, specifically Rome, where it is mentioned in a somewhat different source. The majority of the rabbinic

---

34. This concern would be repeated through the ages. When I was a child, the rabbis did not allow *any* dried fruit to be eaten on Passover because of this fear.
35. *Leket Yosher* 80.

sources I have looked at so far that have discussed haroset have been commentaries of one sort or another, or collections of religious directives. But the *Sefer HeArukh* (The Arranged Book) is different. It is a very early talmudic dictionary, with an entry on haroset. It was written by Rabbi Nathan ben Yehiel at about the same time as Rashi's commentary. He may have been from the same Roman family as the *Shibbolei HaLeket*, but from an earlier generation, as his dictionary was completed in 1101. The *Arukh* is a lexicon of all the talmudic and midrashic terms he thought were in need of explanation. It has always been a valuable resource for students of the Talmud, and has thus been revised and re-edited several times over the centuries. The *Arukh* cites some of the talmudic sources on haroset, and adds that, since in R. Yohanan's opinion it is in memory of clay, it should be made of all sorts of fruits – sweet and bitter – with vinegar, "like clay which has in it everything."

The *Arukh* is quoted in Italian, by a sixteenth-century Roman dictionary, *Tzemah David* (The Shoot of David), by David de Pomis. The editor writes that haroset is a *"mistura fatta con cose dolci et amare, distemperata con aceto, et ridotta in forma di creta,"* i.e., a mixture made with sweet and bitter things, diluted with vinegar, and reduced to the appearance of clay.[36] What is interesting about the *Arukh* is the reference to bitter ingredients as early as the beginning of the twelfth century.

More support for the inclusion of bitter ingredients, specifically bitter herbs, comes from Rabbi Eliezer ben Nathan, of Mainz in Germany, known by the acronym Ravan. He was a contemporary of Rashi's grandsons, and wrote *Even HaEzer* (The Stone of Help), also called *Sefer HaRavan* (The Ravan's Book). In this work of halakha and talmudic commentary he writes about haroset:

> You make haroset with fruits such as apples and nuts and spice and cinnamon and such like, and different sorts of *yerakot* such as *Meerrettich* (horseradish) and lettuce. You must make it acidic or acrid in memory of the apple which is sour, as it is written: "I roused thee under the apple tree" (Song. 8:5), and you must

---

36. D. de Pomis, *Tzemah David: Dittionario Novo Hebraico* (Venice: Ioannes de Gara, 1587), 70r.

make it thick in memory of the mud with which they made the bricks, and the spice is in memory of the straw.[37]

The Ravan stresses the acidity of his haroset here. He lists none of the fruit from the Song of Songs that might have added sweetness, and his apples are definitely sour. He also mentions spice in general, and cinnamon in particular. We have already seen cinnamon in some Sephardic examples of haroset: it was brought from the east by Arab traders, so we first saw it in eleventh-century Fez. Later it appeared in twelfth-century Provençe, thirteenth-century Rome and fourteenth-century Narbonne. Cinnamon now made its appearance in northern European haroset. Indeed, cinnamon was one of the more important spices in all of medieval Europe, an exotic flavoring imported from the Orient. It remains a standard ingredient of Ashkenazic haroset to this day.

But the Ravan's most surprising addition is *Meerrettich*, horseradish, included along with lettuce. It would certainly have given a strong taste to the haroset. Perhaps the Ravan's addition of horseradish was inspired by the Jerusalem Talmud passage that, as we saw in chapter 1, had been corrupted: "And why is it called by the name of *dukkeh*? Because she pounds (*dakhah*) [it] with [him/them/it]." One of the interpretations of this obscure text refers it to bitter herbs: "And why is it called by the name of *dukkeh*? Because it [i.e., the haroset] is pounded with them [i.e., the bitter herbs]."[38]

We have seen that lettuce and other green leafy vegetables were prescribed as *maror*, bitter herbs, in both the Talmuds. The green lettuce leaves, which were probably difficult to obtain in Northern Europe in early spring, were later replaced with horseradish in some Ashkenazic communities. The *Even HaEzer*'s twelfth-century recipe for haroset may have inspired this idea. The substitution of horseradish for lettuce, dated to the fourteenth century, if not earlier, may have been allowed by the rabbis of Ashkenaz because of the similarity in sound between the

37. R Eliezer ben Nathan (1090–c. 1170), *Even HaEzer* (*Sefer Ravan*) (Prague: Moshe Katz, 1610; repr. New York: Grossman, 1958).
38. S. Lieberman, *HaYerushalmi Kifshuto*, vol. I (Jerusalem: Darom, 2008, 3rd ed.), 520, reads this text as saying that it (haroset) must be ground with it (i.e. *maror*).

German word *Meerrettich*, horseradish, and the Aramaic word *merirta*, bitter herbs,[39] and the similarity of both words to the Hebrew *mar*, bitter.

The Ravan's grandson, Rabbi Eliezer ben Joel HaLevi (Ravia), of Bonn, Germany, wrote about haroset in his *Sefer Ravia* (Ravia's Book) at the end of the twelfth century.[40] *Sefer Ravia* does not include *Meerrettich*, horseradish, in the haroset, but it does list flowing myrrh, *mordror*, which is aromatic and slightly bitter.[41] *Mordror* does not appear in any other haroset recipe I have encountered (though *mor*, myrrh, does appear once). Myrrh, however, is mentioned often in the Song of Songs, and, as we saw in chapter 1, flowing myrrh appears in Exodus 30:23 as an ingredient in the Tabernacle incense. The Hebrew letters for *Meerrettich*, מירתיך, and *mordror*, מורדדור, are similar and could be confused if carelessly written. If so, which came first? Was *Meerrettich* the original, a sharp ingredient in the haroset, which because it was on hand, was eventually adopted as bitter herbs instead of the unavailable fresh lettuce in cold Northern Europe? A later scribe, assuming the presence of spices in haroset, might then have misread *Meerrettich* as the biblical *mordror*. Or was it the other way round? Perhaps Ravan, like his grandson, actually wrote that one should put *mordror*, an ingredient of biblical incense, in the haroset, but a later scribe or typesetter, already familiar with *Meerrettich* as bitter herbs, read this back into the earlier recipe. We can no longer be certain. But some rabbis clearly wanted their haroset to be biting as well as acidic.

Rabbi Elazar ben Judah of Worms, a leader of the early mystical Hasidim of Ashkenaz, adds a number of new aspects to haroset. His book, *Sefer HaRoke'aḥ* (The Book of the Perfumer or Apothecary),[42]

---

39. A. Schaffer, "The History of the Horseradish as the Bitter Herb of Passover," *Gesher* 8 (1981): 217–37, attributes the first permission to use horseradish as bitter herbs to Rabbi Alexander Suslin of Frankfurt (d. 1394). See also J. Cooper, *Eat and Be Satisfied: A Social History of Jewish Food* (Northvale/London: Jason Aronson, 1993), 116.

40. Eliezer ben Joel HaLevi (1140–1225), *Sefer Ravia*, vol. 2 (Jerusalem: Makhon Harry Fischel, 1964), 166.

41. *Mordror* is usually translated "flowing myrrh" but the *Jerusalem Bible* has "pure myrrh."

42. Rabbi Elazar ben Judah (1165–1230), *Sefer HaRoke'aḥ*, ed. S. Schneursohn (Jerusalem: Otzar HaPoskim, 1967).

may refer to the description of the incense in the Tabernacle, and he is generally referred to by its title as "the *Roke'aḥ*." He maintained secret traditions and passed them on from generation to generation, and his works include detailed instructions for creating a *golem,* using holy names. He also wrote poetry, including a poem that tells how, at the time of the Third Crusade, his wife, his two daughters and his son were killed before his eyes and he himself was terribly wounded.[43] Today, he is best known for his work on halakha.

The *Roke'aḥ* is the first authority who insists, in no uncertain terms, that apples and nuts are *the* most important ingredients of haroset. Other rabbis had said that haroset should remind us of apples, as in the midrash on the Song of Songs. This was true, though, only insofar as they are acidic, as in Abbaye's view in the Babylonian Talmud. Maimonides also mentioned the acidity, but left us to infer its source, and clearly, his main concern was the consistency of his haroset, rather than the ingredients.

The *Roke'aḥ* mentions acidity as well as consistency. He, like the Tosafists, says that any of the fruits mentioned in the Song of Songs can be used for haroset – nuts, figs and pomegranates. He goes on to detail spices – pepper and ginger – which do not appear in the Song of Songs, but which were in common use in medieval Europe.[44] Indeed, together with cinnamon and saffron, pepper and ginger were the commonest spices.[45] However, the *Roke'aḥ* makes it clear that the apples are the most important ingredient in haroset together with nuts. This view was implied by Ravia before him, but is now made explicit.

The *Roke'aḥ*'s list of ingredients also includes *Meerrettich,* horseradish, as well as *karpas,* usually green celery or parsley used at the Seder for the first dipping, and additional spices. This is the only haroset recipe we have from this period to mention cumin, which was not a common spice in medieval Europe. However, its appearance together with pepper, ginger and *karpas* (which he notes are pounded with vinegar) reminds

---

43. I. Meiseles, *Shirat HaRoke'aḥ: The Poems of Rabbi Elazar ben Judah of Worms* (Jerusalem: unknown publisher, 1993), 9f.

44. See on this: Laurioux, "Spices" (above, n. 19), 43–76.

45. Freedman, *Out of the East* (above, n. 15), 21.

us of the Greco-Roman *oxyporium* I found in the *Apicius* collection. There, the three spices were combined with rue, a green bitter herb, and dates. Did the author of the Book of the Perfumer/Apothecary have an ancient recipe for haroset/*embamma*/*oxyporium*? It is impossible to tell. However, this novel haroset contains not only apples and spices, but also the vegetables used for dipping – both *karpas* greens and bitter herbs – as ingredients of the dip itself.

In chapter 2, we looked at the haroset of the thirteenth-century Provençal *Sefer Baalei HaAsufot*, probably written by Rabbi Judah ben Jacob Lattes. I mentioned there that it included horseradish. In fact, *Sefer Baalei HaAsufot* begins its account of haroset with bitter herbs, specifically "the roots of *amerfoil* (French for 'bitter leaf') which is called *Meerrettich*, horseradish, in the language of Ashkenaz (German), and *lattuga* (the Romance name for lettuce)." The book, like the *Arukh*, explains that the haroset must be bitter, rather than sour.[46] There is no evidence that *Meerrettich* was used as bitter herbs during this period. On the contrary, Rashi's grandson Rabbenu Tam had ruled that it was forbidden to use roots rather than leaves for the bitter herbs, and the first evidence for using *Meerrettich* as bitter herbs comes from the mid-fourteenth century. The single extant manuscript of *Sefer Baalei HaAsufot* is most unclear, and may well contain errors and later additions to the original text. Even so, lettuce was certainly a bitter herb, already listed in the Mishna. The Ravan had made it an ingredient in his haroset, and so did the *Sefer Baalei HaAsufot*, adding the explanation that it serves to remind us of the bitter herbs.

This is the last time we find *Meerrettich* and lettuce as ingredients of haroset in Ashkenaz, although we will find more haroset recipes in both Ashkenaz and Sepharad that include a reminder of the bitter herbs. This development led naturally to the need to make haroset sweet to counteract the bitterness, or acidity.

---

46. The description of haroset is on p. 226 of Gaster's edition. However, there is a problem here with the translation in the text of *amerfoil* as *Meerrettich*, since a few pages earlier (221), *amerfoil* was translated as horehound (*agrorin*, German *andorn*), not as *Meerrettich*, in the context of the bitter herbs, not of haroset. It has, however, been suggested that perhaps *amerfoil* was just a generic name for any sort of bitter herbs.

HAROSET AND BLOOD

Death and Redemption

The symbolic foods of the Seder commemorate both the harsh conditions of the Jewish slaves and their redemption from Egypt. The unleavened matza is the "bread of affliction," the bitter herbs signify the bitterness of slavery and the salt water is interpreted as symbolizing the tears shed by the Jewish slaves. Eating these foods at the Seder incorporates both the memories of the suffering of the Jews in Egypt and their redemption in the past, and connects us with the suffering of Jews over the centuries, as well as foreshadowing the redemption to come. Haroset, too, was said to be a memory of the clay used for the bricks made by the slaves, or alternatively a memory of the apple tree, which is connected to the redemption.

The Jerusalem Talmud saw haroset as symbolizing blood, but did not specify which blood. I have already suggested some possibilities. The first of the ten plagues sent by God to Egypt turned all the water in the land to blood, while the blood of the paschal lamb was painted on the doorposts of Jewish houses as a sign for the Destroyer to pass over them and kill only the firstborn of the Egyptians during the tenth and final plague. There is also the blood of the Israelite children slain by Pharaoh, and the blood of circumcision, referred to by the verse "In thy blood: Live!" (Ezek. 16:6), recited as part of the Haggada. Thus haroset as a symbol of blood contains allusions to both death and redemption.[47]

The agony of the Egyptian slavery is expanded on in various midrashim. The earliest of these is found in the *Targum*, or Aramaic translation of the Bible, on the Book of Exodus, probably written down in the fourth century.[48] In the Book of Exodus, after the redemption from Egypt and the revelation on Mount Sinai, the Jewish people accept the "book of the covenant" of God's laws, declaring, "All that the Lord

---

47. There is also a midrash of Pharaoh becoming a leper, and being told by his advisers that the cure was to bathe in the blood of Jewish babies. This midrash has a Christian parallel in the story of Herod's massacre of the innocents. See on this: I. J. Yuval, *Two Nations in Your Womb: Perceptions of Jews and Christians in the Middle Ages* (Berkeley: University of California Press, 2006), ch. 5.

48. I use the conventional dating of *Targum Pseudo-Jonathan* as in G. Stemberger, *Introduction to the Talmud and the Midrash* (Edinburgh: T. & T. Clark, 1996).

has said will we do, and obey." To ratify this covenant, Moses sprinkles them with blood (Ex. 24:1–8). Following this, he and the priests and elders have a vision of God on His throne, with the likeness of a "brick of sapphire" (*livnat hasapir*)[49] under His feet.

To the literal translation of this verse, the *Targum* adds a midrash telling of the terrible experiences of the Egyptian slavery:

> [The brick is] a memorial of the slavery wherewith the Egyptians enslaved the Children of Israel with clay and bricks. There were women treading the clay with their husbands. There was one delicate young woman who was pregnant, and she aborted her fetus and it got trodden in with the clay. [The angel] Gabriel came down and made it into a brick, and going up to the heavens on high set it as a footstool under the throne of the Lord of the World.

The *Targum* poignantly explains that God, too, has His memorials of the Egyptian slavery. It is a story of persecution which resonates through the ages, and rabbis later used the motif of the delicate girl forced into oppressive labor to underline the sufferings of the whole Jewish people.[50] For us, as post-Holocaust readers, the story resonates deeper still.

In the midrash above, the baby is redeemed by the angel and becomes part of the fabric of heaven. But what of the mother? The *Targum* does not tell us any more about her, but the later *Midrash Pirkei DeRabbi Eliezer* develops her story:

> Israel were gathering the straw in the wilderness, and they trod it with their donkeys and their wives and their children.[51] The straw from the wilderness pricked their heels, and the blood came out and mixed with the clay. Rachel, the granddaughter of Shutelah,

---

49. *Jerusalem Bible*: a kind of paved work of sapphire stone.
50. See e.g. B. L. Visotzky, "Most Tender and Fairest of Women: A Study in the Transmission of Aggada," *Harvard Theological Review* 76 (1983): 403–18.
51. As noted in chapter 1, the corrupt text of the Jerusalem Talmud in Pesaḥim 37d has been interpreted as referring to a woman making haroset together with her husband. This may be the source for both the *Targum* and Midrash showing them treading clay together.

was very pregnant, and she trod the clay with her husband, and the fetus came out of her womb and got mixed up in the brick.[52] Her cry rose to the Throne of Glory and the angel Michael went down and took the brick made with the clay and brought it up before the Throne of Glory. That same night the Holy One blessed be He was revealed, and smote all the firstborn of Egypt as it is said: "At midnight the Lord smote all the firstborn" (Ex. 12:29).[53]

This version explicitly links the brick making with blood – the clay for the bricks is mixed with the blood from the heels of the Jewish slaves, working like donkeys, and pricked by the straw. The woman who aborts her child while treading the clay with her husband is here named Rachel, for in the Book of Jeremiah (31:14) it is Rachel who weeps for her children, the Jewish nation:

"Thus says the Lord;
  'A voice was heard in Rama,
  Lamentation and bitter weeping;
  Rachel weeping for her children;
  She refused to be comforted
  For her children, because they are not.'"

And it is Rachel's cry which reaches God on high (the literal translation of "*Rama*" is a high place), together with her unborn child trampled into the clay.

But the prophecy in Jeremiah (31:15–16) ends with words of hope:

"Thus says the Lord;
  Keep thy voice from weeping...
  For thy work shall be rewarded,

---

52. M. M. Epstein has identified a picture of Rachel, her dead baby and the mould for the brick in the fourteenth-century Golden Haggadah: *The Medieval Haggadah: Art, Narrative and Religious Imagination* (New Haven/London: Yale University Press, 2011), 196–7.

53. *Pirkei DeRabbi Eliezer* 48. This Midrash was probably written in the Land of Israel in the eighth or ninth century.

Says the Lord…
And there is hope for thy future,
Says the Lord,
And thy children shall come back again to their own border."

In both the *Targum* and *Pirkei DeRabbi Eliezer* the trampled fetus brings redemption, but in the Midrash it comes in the form of terrible vengeance, the smiting of the Egyptian firstborn, the death of children for the death of Rachel's child. It was this final plague which brought about the redemption from Egypt.

Perhaps it seems far-fetched to associate the death of these Jewish children with haroset, in spite of the explicit references to blood and clay. We might think that haroset can be linked to the biblical text about brick making, but not necessarily to the midrashim above. However, this dark association seems to have been made by the eleventh-century rabbi and poet Joseph HaKatan ben Samuel Tov Elem (Bonfils), from Narbonne in Provence. Among his *yotzrot*, liturgical poems, is one he wrote for *Shabbat HaGadol*, the Great Sabbath which immediately precedes Passover. It describes the preparations for the festival, and includes a reference to haroset:[54]

And why should it [the bitter herbs] be dipped in haroset?
In memory of the clay which a woman treads with her husband.
And why is spice mixed with it like a brick?
In memory of the scattering of the people to gather stubble for straw.

The image in the poem of a woman treading clay *together with her husband* appears nowhere in the biblical or talmudic texts. We know it only from the stories in the *Targum* and the Midrash about the woman whose baby was trodden into the clay.[55]

---

54. H. Zondel and A. L. Gordon, eds., *Siddur Otzar HaTefillot*, vol. 2 (Vilna: unknown publisher, 1910; repr. Tel Aviv/ Jerusalem: unknown publisher, 1960), 250.
55. See on this: I. J. Yuval, "Passover in the Middle Ages," in *Passover and Easter: Origin*

Haroset and the Blood Libels

Before turning to look at the development of haroset in more modern times, I would like to pause for a moment and examine the connection of haroset with the blood libels in medieval Europe.[56]

Joseph Tov Elem was not alone in associating haroset with the blood and death of children. From about the mid-twelfth century, at the yearly Easter celebrations by Christians commemorating the crucifixion of Jesus, accusations of ritual murder of Christian children were leveled at Jewish communities in Europe. Passover often coincided with Easter and, together with anger against the Jews as "Christ killers," came allegations that the Jews were baking the blood of Christian children into their matza.[57] These blood libels often had tragic consequences. Rabbi Mordechai ben Hillel, the *Mordekhai*, a great-great-grandson of Ravia and a student of the *Or Zarua*, his wife Selda and their five children were among the Jews martyred at Nuremberg in the Rindfleisch massacres in 1298, following blood libels at Mainz and other towns in Germany.

An early blood libel in Savoie, France, in 1329 ended in acquittal for the Jews involved, as their evidence had been given under torture. The Jews of Arles were also accused, in 1453, of killing Christian children and making haroset with their blood. Fortunately, the case was brought before the King, *le bon roi* René, who gave them a fair hearing, and the Jews of Arles were cleared of the baseless accusation.

The Latin protocols of the Savoie trial are still extant, and they detail the revolting accusations about haroset: "The Jews handed over the said children to be killed, and made their heads and intestines into a paste or food which was called *aharace* (haroset) which was made for all the Jews to eat, and which said food the said Jews eat at Passover instead

---

and *History to Modern Times*, ed. P. F. Bradshaw and L. A. Hoffman (Notre Dame: Notre Dame University Press, 1999), 127–60, esp. 153–4, and in more detail in *Two Nations* (above, n. 47), 248–54. Yuval does not mention the *Targum*, only the Midrash.

56. For a more detailed study of haroset and the blood libels, see my paper "'In Thy Blood, Live!' Haroset and the Blood Libels," *Revue des Études Juives* 172, 1–2 (2013): 83–100.

57. The first accusation of ritual murder against Jews took place in Norwich in England in 1140.

of the Passover sacrifice."[58] The protocols accuse Jews in every part of the world of making their haroset, which they call *"aharace,"* on Passover in certain years from these ingredients, which, they believe, will bring salvation. They then record the accusation that Acelin the Jew ate this *aharace*, together with a Christian accomplice, who admitted to selling him two Christian children.

Acelin was forced to defend himself and the whole Jewish community against these charges. In his defense, also preserved in the protocols, he declared that he had never bought children, and that the Jews never mixed blood or meat in their *aharace*. This was against the Law given them by Moses. Jews, instead, were required to put unleavened bread and wild lettuce in their *aharace*.[59] The judge acquitted the accused and the local Jewish community. But for Acelin it was too late. He died in prison as a result of the torture he had suffered.

These two cases demonstrate clearly that when medieval Christians accused Jews of using blood in their preparations for Passover, they were also referring to haroset.[60] Blood was not mentioned in the written accusation, but from the Jewish refutation it is clear that the Jews were aware that blood was part of the ritual murder fantasy, which they denied. Acelin declared that Jews "never mixed blood or meat in their *aharace.*"

But accusations of ritual murder did not stop in the Middle Ages. In seventeenth-century Cracow, Rabbi David ben Samuel HaLevi, author of the *Turei HaZahav* (The Rows [or Columns] of Gold, and known by the acronym of its title as the *Taz*), instructed his community not to use red wine at their Passover Seder. He had lived through the Chmielnicki massacres in 1649, and feared that the wine would be taken for blood. Perhaps this is the reason that no present-day Ashkenazic communities I found dilute their haroset with red wine at the table.

---

58. Text from: M. Esposito, "Un process contre les Juifs de la Savoie en 1329," *Revue d'histoire écclesiastique* 34 (1938), 785–95. The translation is my own.
59. R. Ben Shalom, "The Ritual Murder Accusation at Arles and the Franciscan Mission at Avignon in 1453," *Zion* 63 (1996 [Hebrew]): 391–407. The original Latin texts are given by M. Esposito (above, n. 58). It is interesting to note that the Florentine scholar Esposito failed to identify the nature of *aharace*. It was identified by B. Z. Dinur, *Israel in the Diaspora*, vol. 2.2 (Tel Aviv/Jerusalem: Dvir, 1966 [Hebrew]), 556.
60. Ben Shalom (art. cit., n. 59 above), 399.

Indeed, accusations that Jews murdered Christians for their Seder rituals persisted for centuries. (The poet Hayim Nahman Bialik wrote two poems on the Kishinev blood libel and subsequent pogrom in 1903.) In one of the most notorious cases of blood libel, the so-called "Damascus Affair" in 1840, a group of Syrian Jews were accused of having murdered a friar. They were imprisoned and tortured. One died, one converted to Islam and the rest were freed only after the personal intervention of Sir Moses Montefiore, a British Jew, who intervened on behalf of Jewish communities all over the world. The British newspapers gave the case wide coverage. On August 17, 1840, *The Times* in London even printed a translation of most of the Haggada on its front page, in order to "repel strongly the barbarous notion that human blood, or blood of any kind, is essential to its celebration."[61] *The Times* also provided details of what haroset is *actually* made from. It is, they wrote, "a compound formed of almonds and apples worked up to the consistency of lime, in memory of the bricks and water on which they laboured in Egypt" ("water" is clearly a mistake and meant to be "mortar").

Sir Moses himself was born in Livorno, in Italy, although he ended his life in England. His wife Judith was most probably the author of the first English Jewish cookery book. We shall meet her again in happier circumstances in chapter 5.

---

61. Y. H. Yerushalmi, *Haggadah and History* (Philadelphia: Jewish Publication Society of America, 1975), 77 and pl. 95.

Chapter 4

Moving Toward Modernity

Put a little ground pottery in the haroset in memory of the clay. I was astounded to see something as crazy as this – maybe now on the festival of Purim they will go in for bloodletting in memory of the edict to exterminate all the Jews? Surely we are meant to turn misery into rejoicing and the bad to good.

Rabbi Menahem of Lonzano, as quoted by the Hida

Throughout much of their history, Jewish communities have been mobile.[1] Sometimes their migrations were the result of persecutions, such as when Jews were expelled from Spain in 1492, while at other times they were the result of the lifting of restrictive laws, such as when Jews moved to England after the fall of the Catholic monarchy in the seventeenth century. When they moved, the Jews took their traditions with them, and sometimes these traditions differed from the local customs of their new communities. It is also clear that there were often tensions

---

1. For an overview of Jewish migrations: S. M. Lowenstein, *The Jewish Cultural Tapestry: International Jewish Folk Traditions* (Oxford/NY, 2000).

between the rabbis and the lay people, some of whom evidently went their own way, and whose newfangled customs could only be ratified in retrospect. Rabbinical control over haroset gradually began to weaken.

At the same time, conflicts began to develop among the rabbis themselves. Rabbis have always disagreed and argued among themselves, as is clear already from the time of the Mishna. As long as such argument was "in the name of heaven," it was not problematic, and could often be fruitful. But sometimes disagreement became bitter conflict, and the disputants did not always control their language. In this chapter, I begin by looking at some disagreements over the changing ingredients of haroset.

One way of coping with the changing ingredients was to rise above them. In this chapter, I shall therefore explore how the rabbis came to attribute kabbalistic and messianic symbolism to their haroset, so that the ingredients became simply a means to a higher goal.

THE RASHBATZ: DATES AND CINNAMON

An early example of new trends and new ways of looking at the traditional haroset ingredients may be found in the writings of Rabbi Simeon ben Tzemah Duran (Rashbatz), a fourteenth-century rabbi from the island of Majorca, known for his individualist stance on a number of issues.[2] He represents a new trend which denies eroticism, but he makes use of the exotic and the mythological in his interpretation.

As we saw in chapter 2, the first definitive record of the ingredients in haroset came from Rav Amram Gaon in Babylonia. "In our part of the world," he wrote, "we make it from dates." The Ashkenazic Tosafists quoted the Sephardic *Geonim* when they gave rabbinical authority to dates, explaining that haroset should be made from fruits in the Song of Songs that allegorize the Jewish people. These included dates, based on the words of the lover to his beloved, "I will go up into the palm tree" (Song. 7:8).

Many rabbis followed them in quoting this erotic allusion in relation to haroset, but not the Rashbatz. He quoted instead a verse from

---

2. Rabbi Simeon ben Tzemah Duran (Rashbatz, 1361–1444) lived first in Palma de Majorca, then in Algiers. He wrote about haroset in his *Book About Leaven* (*Sefer Maamar Ḥametz*) (Livorno, 1744; repr. Jerusalem: Makhon Ḥatam Sofer, 1970).

the Book of Psalms which is recited in the synagogue every Sabbath: "The righteous man flourishes like the palm tree" (Ps. 92:13). He does not explain his departure from the traditional interpretation, but if we look at his discussion of the apples in haroset we can perhaps understand why:

> It says in Tractate Sota [in the Babylonian Talmud] that the modest daughters of Israel used to go to their husbands in secret, so that the Egyptians would not be aware. They would tempt their husbands with mirrors of glass and get pregnant under the apple trees, as it is said: "I roused thee under the apple tree; there thy mother was in travail with thee; there she who bore thee was in travail" (Song. 8:5). And they gave birth there and there were thousands [of babies].... Because of this, those mirrors were chosen to make the basin in which to check the women accused of adultery who had left the paths of modesty. And in memory of that you make the haroset from the apples.[3]

The Rashbatz was noticeably concerned with the subject of modesty in sexual relations. Previous rabbis had nothing but praise for the women who tempted their husbands under the apple tree, but the Rashbatz appears uncomfortable with their actions. He asserts that, because women have been known to tempt men other than their husbands, the mirrors used by the Israelite women were later used as part of the ceremony for investigating the *sota*, the woman accused of adultery by her husband. Perhaps because of his concern over temptresses, the Rashbatz refrains from quoting those particularly erotic verses about the date palm, even if they are from the Song of Songs.

Similarly, when talking about the spices for haroset, the Rashbatz makes an association with the incense offered in the Temple, rather than citing previous associations with the spices in the Song of Songs. Although, as we have seen, earlier commentators had alluded to some of the ingredients of the incense in the Tabernacle, particularly flowing myrrh, *mordror*, and "all the chief spices," the Rashbatz was the first to

---

3. Rashbatz (above, n. 2), 35.

explicitly link the cinnamon in the incense used in the Temple to the cinnamon in haroset.[4]

He cites some beautiful midrashim about cinnamon, which tell us that some of the spices used in the Temple incense actually grew in Jerusalem and will grow there once again, when the Messiah comes. He quotes Song of Songs Rabba, the Midrash on Song of Songs,[5] which says that cinnamon used to grow in Jerusalem. Goats and deer would graze on it, and when the people used it as fuel to light their ovens, its fragrance spread all over the Land of Israel. But when Jerusalem was destroyed, the cinnamon disappeared, apart from a tiny piece that was preserved in the treasury of a legendary Queen named Tzimtzemai.[6]

I have already noted the function of food in inscribing and incorporating memories, especially at the Seder, where it serves to create and underline Jews' memories of their history. By eating matza and bitter herbs, Jews throughout the ages identified with the bitter memories of Egyptian slavery, as well as with all the Jews of previous generations who had eaten these foods at Passover. When haroset was added to the Seder ceremony, the rabbis used it to conjure up collective memories, as we have seen. The spices of the Rashbatz's haroset brought with them nostalgia for a mythical Golden Age when the Temple still stood and the air was perfumed with cinnamon.

Song of Songs Rabba continues and takes us back further still, to the cradle of Jewish myth, to the Garden of Eden itself, and the redemption after the Flood. On the verse from the Song of Songs, "Thou hast doves' eyes" (Song. 4:1), the Midrash explains:

Just as the dove brought light to the world, so Israel brings light to the world...

When did the dove bring light to the world?

---

4. The Babylonian Talmud had given details of the incense and its spices, in a passage which is now part of the Sabbath liturgy: Keritot 6a.
5. The Midrash on the Song of Songs begins with the word Ḥazita, "Can you see?" Thus it is often called *Midrash Ḥazita* by Jewish writers, and Rashbatz cites it as such.
6. Rashbatz is referring here to Shabbat 63a and Y. Pe'ah 20a. Queen Tzimtzemai appears in the Rashbatz's source in the Babylonian Talmud, but nowhere else.

In the days of Noah, as it says: "And the dove came in to him in the evening; and, lo, in her mouth was an olive leaf plucked off" (Gen. 8:11)...

Where did she bring it from?...

R. Tarye said: "The gates of the Garden of Eden were opened to her and she brought it from there."

R. Aibu said to him: "Had she brought it from the Garden of Eden she should have brought something better, like cinnamon or balsam. But in fact she gave him a hint, saying: 'Noah, better is bitterness from this source [=God], than sweetness from your hand.'"

But cinnamon for the Rashbatz is not merely a memory of mythical times. In a lengthy discussion of the spices for haroset, he also attempts to identify this spice, bringing various names and botanical affiliations in Latin and Arabic. He disagrees with Maimonides' identification,[7] and writes:

It would seem that the cinnamon which is mentioned in the laws of Passover is the spice or perfume which is a sort of bark.... The choice part of this is called *dar Tzini*, the tree which comes from the land of *Tzin* (China), for *dar* is tree in the language of *Kedar* (Arabic) and *dar Tzini* is the tree which comes from the land of *Tzin*.

Dar Tzini is, in fact, the Arabic for cassia, often confused with cinnamon in the Middle Ages.[8]

I have already noted the immense popularity of spices in the Middle Ages. One of the reasons for this was their exotic nature. They came from faraway lands like China and India, and were thus both costly and desirable. In the medieval imagination of both Jews and Christians,

---

7. The Rashbatz is referring to Maimonides' discussion of cinnamon in the context of the incense in the Temple, not haroset: *Hilkhot Klei HaMikdash* 1:3.

8. Ibn Baytar and his discussion of what he calls *"dar Sini"* is noted by N. Nasrallah, *Annals of the Caliphs' Kitchens: Ibn Sayyar al-Warraq's Tenth-Century Baghdadi Cookbook* (Leiden/Boston: Brill, 2010), 649.

India, the source of many spices, was conceived of as bordering on the Garden of Eden, the earthly paradise.[9] Rashbatz's haroset summoned up the earliest, mythical times. But his evident enjoyment of the exotic and faraway is expressed not only in these intimations of Eden and its exotic scents, but also in the use of exotic languages in his discussion of the Chinese origins of *dar Tzini*, cinnamon (or cassia). Just as the taste of his haroset is enhanced by the addition of spices brought from afar, so his textual tradition is enriched by the citation of foreign tongues relating to the farthest East. Finally, for the Rashbatz, haroset also foretells the taste of the Messianic Age, when cinnamon will again grow wild around Jerusalem and the righteous will flourish like a date palm.

HAROSET DISPUTES

Rabbinic debate about the ingredients in haroset continued. I have noted that the tenth-century *Arukh* seems to have been the first source to record the custom of including bitter herbs in haroset. The *Tur*, who moved from Ashkenaz to Sepharad, also followed this custom, and noted that haroset should at least contain sour ingredients in memory of the bitter herbs.

Some rabbis, however, disagreed, among them Rabbi Joseph Caro, author of the *Beit Yosef* (The House of Joseph), a commentary on the *Tur*. Caro's family left Spain after the expulsion in 1492, and were then forced to leave Portugal in 1497. Caro himself moved to Salonica, then Constantinople, before finally ending up in Safed in the Galilee. Here he condensed the *Beit Yosef* into the *Shulḥan Arukh* (The Laid Table), which forms the basis for modern Jewish halakha. Claiming a textual scribal error, the *Beit Yosef* suggests that the *Tur*'s opinion regarding haroset be read as follows: "…of sour ingredients in memory of the apple, as it is written, 'Under the apple tree' (Song. 8:5)."[10] Thus the *Beit Yosef* returns to the view, popular in Ashkenaz, that the acidity of haroset is in memory of the apples.

---

9. P. Freedman, *Out of the East: Spices and the Medieval Imagination* (New Haven/London: Yale University Press, 2008).

10. *Beit Yosef* on the *Tur, Oraḥ Ḥayim, Hilkhot Pesaḥ*, 473.

Facing the *Beit Yosef* on the printed page, and responding to him, just as the Tosafists were in dialogue with Rashi around the text of the Talmud, is the *Bayit Ḥadash* (The New House), the *Baḥ*, written a generation later by Rabbi Joel Sirkis of Cracow. He disagreed with the *Beit Yosef.* The *Baḥ* refused to accept that there was a scribal error in the text of the *Tur*, maintaining that it was far-fetched to resolve substantial arguments by regularly finding fault in available manuscripts.[11] He believed that haroset should be acidic in memory of the bitter herbs, and not in memory of the apple.

The halakha, he says, supports R. Yohanan's opinion in the Talmud, that haroset is in memory of the clay, and not in memory of the apple. Therefore, its acidity cannot be in memory of the apple. The reason for apples, says the *Baḥ*, followed the opinion of the Tosafot, which included fruits to which the Children of Israel are compared in the Song of Songs. Apples in haroset, like figs and nuts, serve merely as an allusion to the redemption from Egypt. The *Baḥ* also objected to adding pomegranates and dates, because they are not associated specifically with the redemption, and in particular he objected to adding almonds, which are mentioned by the prophet Jeremiah (1:11–16) in the context of a prophecy of punishment to come. Perhaps, we might add, although he does not say so, that dates and pomegranates were not readily available in sixteenth-century Cracow. The *Baḥ*, however, was fighting a losing battle. In spite of his long and closely reasoned argument, apples were becoming the most important ingredient in Ashkenazic haroset.

A generation later still, Rabbi Joseph ben David wrote his halakhic work *Beit David* (House of David), which was published posthumously in Turkish-ruled Salonica, in 1740.[12] Like some of his predecessors, the *Beit David* related to the question of including bitter herbs in haroset. He points out that this custom appears only in the *Arukh,* and not in the

---

11. Traditional rabbinical learning uses the Yiddish term *kvetch* to translate *daḥuk*, which I have translated "far-fetched."

12. Rabbi Joseph ben David (1662–1736), *Beit David* (Salonica: Betzalel Ashkenazi Press, 1740). Rabbi Joseph is more famous for his work *Tzemaḥ David* (The Shoot of David) on the Torah.

talmudic texts or Maimonides, but that the *Tur* and Maimonides had said to include sour ingredients in memory of the bitter slavery.

The *Beit David* recalls that Rashi had said to put *yerakot*, green herbs or vegetables, in haroset in order to thicken it. Perhaps, he suggests, in some communities participants would put the bitter herbs and the other herbs used at the Seder into the haroset. After all, the *Arukh* had written that haroset is made "of sweet and bitter kinds, like clay which has a little of everything in it." The *Beit David*, however, condemns the Jews of Salonica for omitting sour ingredients from their haroset. It is clear that he feels that matters are slipping beyond control, for he stresses that not using sour elements expressly contravenes the instructions of the Talmud.

Greens, *yerakot*, are also mentioned as an ingredient of haroset by Rabbi Hayim Joseph David Azulai, the Hida (1724–1806), in his children's book on Passover, *Simhat HaRegel* (The Joy of the Pilgrim Festival), which he wrote when he was himself a young man.[13] The Hida describes a minimalist haroset, made of the most basic and least expensive ingredients – green vegetables and water – though he still insists on something acidic, and stringy bits of spice.

In early Ashkenaz, several rabbis, in particular the *Leket Yosher*, began to restrict the use of dried figs and raisins in haroset because they might have come into contact with flour, which could ferment on contact with water and turn to leaven. It is clear, however, that in the border countries of Provence and Italy, a wide variety of ingredients, including figs, were still in use, and we shall see in the next chapter that they continued to be used in some Sephardic communities.

By the late sixteenth to the early seventeenth century, this discrepancy between Ashkenazic and Sephardic haroset caused problems for the rabbis. Rabbi Yom Tov Lipman Heller was a rabbi in Prague and Vienna who wrote a supercommentary on the commentary of the Italian Bartenura on Mishna Pesahim, called *Tosefot Yom Tov* (Yom Tov's

---

13. Hayim Joseph David ben Isaac Azulai, *Simhat HaRegel* (Livorno: A. I. Castillio & A. Saadon, 1781): title page: "Written by myself, the young Hayim Joseph David ben Isaac Azulai … for Jewish children."

Additions).[14] Noting that the Bartenura mentions apples, figs and hazel-nuts as ingredients of his haroset, he points out that the talmudic text did not include figs or hazelnuts. "I do not know where he got this from," he writes. There is indeed no authority for hazelnuts, although they were commonly in use in the Spanish and Italian traditions by this time. Pre-sumably figs were less used in Germany after the ban by the *Leket Yosher*. There was solid authority for them, however, from the Tosafists, who interpreted the verse about figs in the Song of Songs, "the fig tree puts forth her green figs" (Song. 2:13), as a metaphor for the Jewish people. Perhaps the *Tosefot Yom Tov* was trying to avoid controversy.

Hazelnuts and figs also appear in another interesting recipe from the Spanish Diaspora, which demonstrates how the disparate traditions came to influence each other. I noted above how the family of Rabbi Joseph Caro fled to Portugal, after the expulsion from Spain in 1492, and then to Turkey. Many other Sephardic Jewish refugees made their way to the more tolerant religious atmosphere of the Netherlands, and from there to England, where they were finally allowed entrance in 1656. The archives of London's oldest surviving synagogue, Bevis Marks, preserve a Sephardic recipe for haroset from 1726, with raisins, almonds, cinnamon, pistachios, dates, ginger, walnuts, apples, pears, figs and hazelnuts.[15] The last recipes for haroset we saw from London from before the expulsion from England in 1290 were completely Ashkenazic in character. This one, imported together with the new Sephardic community, has a distinctly Spanish flavor, with the addition of ginger, pistachios and hazelnuts.

Yet another haroset recipe with hazelnuts comes from an Italian Haggada, written entirely in Spanish. After the decree of expulsion from Spain, many Jews indeed left, but some who stayed formally converted to Christianity to avoid persecution, while secretly preserving their Judaism. Throughout the centuries, their descendants continued to flee, sometimes at the risk of their lives, to places where they could live openly as Jews. Livorno/Leghorn in Italy was one of the places willing to

---

14. Rabbi Yom Tov Lipman ben Nathan HaLevi Heller (1579–1654), *Tosefot Yom Tov* on Mishna Pesaḥim 10:3.
15. J. Cooper, *Eat and Be Satisfied: A Social History of Jewish Food* (New Jersey/London: Jason Aronson, 1993), 135.

take them in, and a community of Spanish-speaking Jews grew up there. Forced for years to practice their Judaism in secret, these transplanted Jews needed to learn more about their religion once they were free to do so. They had little or no knowledge of Hebrew, however, and a literature for teaching them was produced, often in Spanish or Portuguese. The Jewish Theological Seminary library in New York has a Haggada written for these former crypto-Jews, or Marranos, in Livorno in 1654. The title page provides the background to its publication: "The order of the Haggada for the night of the festival of Passover, translated from the original Hebrew, conforming to that which our sages ordained... printed at the request and expense of David [son] of Jacob Valençin."[16] A recipe for *el Arosset* appears on the final page:

> Take apples or pears, cooked in water: hazelnuts or almonds: shelled chestnuts or walnuts: figs or raisins: and after cooking, grind them thoroughly and dissolve them in the strongest wine vinegar that can be found. Then mix in a bit of brick dust, in memory of the bricks which our fathers made in Egypt. For eating, cinnamon powder is sprinkled above. Those who wish to add other fruits and spices into the concoction may do so.[17]

This haroset recipe reflects a decidedly northern Ashkenazic influence with its apples and pears, but it is otherwise flexible in its ingredients, with Italian roots evident in its four varieties of nuts, including chestnuts and hazelnuts.

Most interesting, perhaps, is the inclusion in this Livorno recipe of "a bit of brick dust." As we saw earlier, it was the *Shibbolei HaLeket* from Rome who first mentioned grit or ground potsherds as an ingredient of haroset. The use of grit as an ingredient in haroset is also recorded in Salonica. The *Beit David* had reported the custom of adding ground

---

16. D. Valençin, *Orden dela Hagadah de noche de Pascoa de Pesah. Tradusida dela original Hebraica conforme la ordenaron nuestros Sabios* (Livorno: Gio. Vincenza Bonfigli, 1654).
17. Translation: Y. H. Yerushalmi, *Haggadah and History* (Philadelphia: Jewish Publication Society of America, 1975), pl. 58 and commentary.

potsherds or the grit made from grinding the stone *kailiramini,* which is red, and reminiscent of clay.

Kailiramini probably comes from the Greek *pelos armeni* (Armenian earth), via the Arabic, where "p" was often mixed up with the similar letter "q."[18] This Armenian earth was a viscous red clay used medicinally, for example, as a prophylactic against plague. It was also called *tin armeni* in Arabic, which became *teet armeni* in Hebrew. And haroset, of course, was in memory of *teet,* the clay which was used in brick making in Egypt.

Not everyone approved of this custom. Rabbi Menahem of Lonzano was a kabbalist and textual scholar who made use of many manuscripts to establish and publish the most accurate versions of the text of the Torah, the Zohar and Midrashim. He also added new entries to the *Arukh.* However, he made many personal enemies, and as a result died in poverty.[19] His vehement diatribe against putting grit into haroset is quoted by the Hida in another of his works, the *Birkei Yosef:*[20]

> *Put a little ground pottery in the haroset in memory of the clay.*
> I was astounded to see something as crazy as this – maybe now on the festival of Purim they will go in for bloodletting in memory of the edict to exterminate all the Jews? Surely we are meant to turn misery into rejoicing and the bad to good.

Rabbi Menahem identifies the source of this custom, which he renders ridiculous with his incisive sarcasm, in a scribal error. Rashi, he says, writes about crushing haroset finely in memory of clay. In some manuscripts, however, there was clearly a mistake (or perhaps an abbreviation). Instead of the words, "*ḥaroset* חר[ו]סת which they crush finely,"

---

18. G. Bos et al., *Medical Synonym Lists for Medieval Provence: Shem Tov ben Isaac of Tortosa: Sefer HaShimmush. Book 29,* Part 1 (Leiden: Brill, 2011). I am grateful to Gerrit Bos for his help in elucidating these terms.

19. Rabbi Menahem ben Judah, the Ram or Maharam MiLonzano (1550–before 1624). Rabbi Menahem seems to have had a MS copy of the *Shibbolei HaLeket:* J. S. Penkower, "A Note Regarding R. Menahem de Lonzano": http://seforim.blogspot.co.il/2009/08/jordan-s-penkower-note-regarding-r.html (accessed April 2018).

20. Hayim Joseph David Azulai, *Sefer Birkei Yosef* (The Lap [lit. Knees] of Joseph) (Livorno: G. V. Falorni, 1774; repr. Jerusalem: Makhon Ḥatam Sofer, 1969).

the text reads, "*heres* חרס (potsherd) which they crush finely." This, indeed, is the version quoted by the *Tosefot Yom Tov*.[21] Recently, Rabbi David Golinkin made the interesting suggestion that what might seem like a scribal error was, in fact, a deliberate attempt to "concretize" the slavery of the Jews in Egypt.[22] Indeed, we noted in chapter 3 that the sixteenth-century German convert Margaritha reported that Jews made their haroset in the shape, *Gestalt*, of a brick. Golinkin cites an episode from 1862 in support of his claim, when Jewish soldiers in the American Civil War made a Seder in the mountains of West Virginia. Since they had none of the ingredients for haroset, they put a real brick in its place on their Seder table.[23]

In spite of the considerable authority of the Hida, finely crushed *heres* (potsherd) or brick dust or even crushed stone became an ingredient of haroset in Salonica and elsewhere. The use of ground potsherds is prescribed even in some more recent Haggadas, and is proudly continued by some families to this day.

Another ingredient still subject to controversy at this time was the chestnut. We have already seen this as an ingredient of haroset in the border lands of Northern Italy and Provence, where it grew wild or cost very little. It was clearly used in Salonica too, but the *Beit David* disapproved. Chestnuts, he says, "are not mentioned in any verse, and we have not found that the Jewish people are ever compared to chestnuts." He is right, of course, but the Hida did not miss the opportunity to disagree with him yet again. He quotes the authority of the *Sefer HaMenuha*, which, as we have seen, reported it as a local custom in thirteenth-century Italy. In his *Simhat HaRegel*, the Hida described a

---

21. The standard edition of the Talmud, the *Vilna Shas*, has the reading *heres*, rather than *haroset*, in the text of the Rashbam, not Rashi, on Pesahim 116a. The marginal notes known as *Masoret HaShas*, which were added in the eighteenth century, write that *heres* in the text of the Rashbam "should be *haroset*."
22. D. Golinkin, "Pesah Potpourri: On the Origin and Development of Some Lesser-Known Pesah Customs," *Conservative Judaism* 55/3 (2003): 58–71, esp. 63.
23. See on this: http://onthemainline.blogspot.co.il/2013/02/pesach-is-in-air-so-civil-war-seder-1862.html (accessed April 2018), which also cites the children's book written about this episode: B. J. Fireside, S. Costello, *Private Joel and the Sewell Mountain Seder* (Minneapolis: Kar-Ben Publishing, 2008).

minimalist and inexpensive haroset based mainly on vegetables and water. Here, in his *Birkei Yosef,* he once again takes care not to exclude a cheap, perhaps even free, ingredient.

All three ingredients which we have seen as controversial – pears, chestnuts and grit – continued to be used in eighteenth-century Italy. The evidence for this comes from an unusual source, the *Lexicon Chaldaico-Rabbinicum,* a Rabbinic Aramaic Dictionary in Latin compiled by a Christian Hebraist, Antonio Zanolini, in Padua in 1747. Zanolini translates haroset as the Greek *embamma,* and adds a vernacular name, *mostarda.* He is presumably referring to *mostarda veneta,* which *The Oxford Companion to Italian Food* describes as "a thick cooked paste made with quinces, apples and pears, and flavored with sugar and mustard."[24] Zanolini notes that haroset was originally made of dates, raisins and figs mixed with vinegar and spice. In his discussion of the paschal lamb he quotes "Majemonidis," and his first record of haroset mirrors Maimonides' haroset from the *Mishneh Torah.* In his day, however, Zanolini tells us, the *Hebraei,* the Jews, "grind apples, pears, chestnuts with sugar and other spices in a mortar and with vinegar mix in a lump of a certain mud…recalling cement, to which they add cinnamon on top."[25] We may wonder whether the other spices included mustard.

Thus having set up a standard for haroset as sour and clay-like, the rabbis increasingly discovered, as they moved into the early modern period, that the specific ingredients were beginning to escape their control. Alternative local traditions were growing and proliferating. The apple was taking over as the main ingredient in Ashkenaz, where bitter herbs were disappearing, while in the Sephardic world, outsider ingredients such as pistachios, hazelnuts, chestnuts and even grit were being used, without the stamp of rabbinical approval.

24. G. Riley, *The Oxford Companion to Italian Food* (Oxford: Oxford University Press, 2007).
25. A. Zanolini, *Lexicon Chaldaico-Rabbinicum* (Padua: Typis Seminarii, 1747): *maror*: 263; *seh,* lamb: 696–700.

KABBALISTIC AND REDEMPTIVE HAROSET

Some early modern rabbis were not interested in the ingredients of haroset as such. For them, these were merely a stepping stone to a greater significance beyond the here and now. From its earliest appearance, haroset was meant to inscribe and incorporate Jewish memories of the slavery in Egypt. We saw how the Rashbatz saw haroset and its spices as an allusion to earlier, even mythical times – the Garden of Eden, the Golden Age when the Temple still stood – and to future Messianic times.

The rise of the kabbalists in the sixteenth century produced further mystical interpretations. The name "haroset" and the names of the ingredients themselves were taken and used by them in spiritual word games. The first of these was an Ashkenazic bilingual word play based on both the holy language, Hebrew, and the secular German. It is traced, surprisingly, to Rabbi Isaac Luria, a Sephardic rabbi, with Ashkenazic antecedents. Known as HaAri HaKadosh (the Holy Lion, after the initials of HaElohi Rabbi Isaac, the divine Rabbi Isaac), he was a rabbi, a poet and a leading kabbalist.[26] Born in Jerusalem, he lived for some time in Egypt, studying in seclusion on an island in the Nile before moving back to the Land of Israel, where he became the leader of a group of kabbalists in Safed in Upper Galilee. Safed, indeed, now became one of the four Jewish holy towns, the home of the spiritual.[27] The Ari lived in Safed for only two years before dying in an epidemic at the age of thirty-eight, but his influence on later Judaism has been enormous.

The Ari is quoted by his kabbalist pupil, Rabbi Hayim Vital, in his book of mystical explanations of the halakhot, the *Peri Etz Ḥayim* (The Fruit of the Tree of Life), based mainly on the Ari's oral teachings. Rabbi Hayim cites the Ari as talking about "haroset *ev"en* and haroset *e"tz*."[28]

---

26. Rabbi Isaac Luria (1534–1572) is sometimes called the Arizal, the divine Rabbi Isaac, z"l, may his memory be blessed.
27. Each of the holy towns, Jerusalem, Tiberias, Hebron and Safed, was associated with one of the four medieval "elements," fire, water, earth and air. Jerusalem, which was burned down, will arise again in fire; Tiberias, on the Sea of Galilee, is associated with water; Hebron, site of the Tombs of the Patriarchs, stands for earth; while Safed, home of the spiritual, is air.
28. Rabbi Hayim Vital, *Sefer Peri Etz Ḥayim: Sha'ar Ḥag HaMatzot*, chapter 6, from the version on the CD-ROM of HaTaklitor HaTorani.

Haroset, according to the Ari, is made mainly from three ingredients – apples, pears and nuts – whose initial letters in German (or, as he calls it, "the language of Ashkenaz") – *Apfel, Biren, Nüsse* – spell the word *ev"en* (*ab"n*), "stone" in Hebrew. We saw in chapter 3 that fifteenth-century German illustrated Haggadas show these ingredients, and that the sixteenth-century convert Margaritha in Augsburg mentioned "haroset *ev"en*." The Ari develops this idea further, adding that the initial letters of the German names for two traditional spices, *Ingbar* and *Tzimmerind*, ginger and cinnamon, become the mnemonic *e"tz* (*i"tz*), wood in Hebrew.

It is curious indeed to find a Sephardic rabbi citing an Ashkenazic version of haroset using German vocabulary, and we may wonder about his source. But it seems to me that the mystical significance overrides mundane questions of locality and custom. Haroset *ev"en* and haroset *e"tz* are lisping puns on the biblical phrases *haroshet even* and *haroshet etz*, "the carving of stone and carving of wood," terms used in the Torah to describe the work of building the *Mishkan*, the Tabernacle (Ex. 31:5; 35:33).

The Ari has taken these words, which refer to the Tabernacle, as a reference point for the ingredients of haroset. We have seen how haroset through the ages has been interpreted as a memory of the clay and blood used in the bricks which built the cities of the pagan Egyptians. The Ari transforms the blood-soaked clay used to build idolatrous Egypt into the materials for building the Tabernacle, the earthly home of the *Shekhina*, the seat of the Divine Presence.

This seemingly banal word play is part of an ancient system called *gematria*, numerology, wherein language, words and even individual letters are seen as carrying deep metaphysical significance.[29] Hebrew, according to the Torah, was the language used by God in creating the world. Like the Greeks, Jews attributed a numerical value to each letter of their alphabet, so that words with the same numerical value could be seen

---

29. For a discussion of *gematria*, see the article under this heading in *The Jewish Encyclopedia* (New York, 1906), http://www.jewishencyclopedia.com/articles/6571-gematria (accessed April 2018). Kabbalistic *gematria* is a much wider concept than the mere use of the numerical value of letters.

as related to each other. Similar sounding or similarly written Hebrew words were also seen as related to each other in kabbalistic philology.

These serious verbal games of Seder night were not confined to Ashkenaz. Rabbi David ben Abraham, grandson of the Rambam, also played with words related to haroset. I have already noted that Rav Amram, in the ninth century, called haroset *ḥallika*, and that Jews from Babylonia – modern Iran and Iraq – call haroset *ḥillek* or *ḥallek* to this day. Rabbi David, in thirteenth-century Damascus, noted this tradition and expanded its significance. The word *ḥillek*, he pointed out, comprises the same Hebrew consonants as the word *hekel*, lightened or made easier.[30] The Holy One blessed be He lightened – *hekel* – the burden of Egyptian slavery, collected us and brought us out of Egypt. Thus haroset as *ḥillek* contains within its very letters the memory of God's redemption of the Jewish people from slavery.

Rabbi David does not stop there. After the redemption from Egypt, he writes, God gathered the Jewish people in the wilderness, protecting them with the clouds of His glory, and instructed them to eat the Passover lamb in memory of the redemption. They were to eat it as they ate the original paschal lamb in Egypt, assembled in communal groups, "the whole assembly of the congregation Israel" (Ex. 12:6). *Kahal*, the communal group, also has the same consonants as *ḥillek*, which thus became a memory of redemption for the whole united community, together carrying out the command of their One God.

Later hasidic rabbis also spoke of the mystical meaning behind haroset. Rabbi Nahman ben Simha of Breslov (1772–1811) was a hasidic *tzaddik*, a holy man, who lived in the Ukraine and believed that he was destined to be the Messiah through whom the whole Jewish community could be redeemed.[31] His teachings on nature, faith, joy and melody are currently undergoing a revival, while his tomb in Uman has become the focal point of mass pilgrimage, particularly at Rosh HaShana, the New Year. A magical letter-triangle based on his name is found in graffiti all over present-day Israel, from Dan to Beersheva:

---

30. *Ḥillek* is actually written with an initial letter *ḥet*, while *hekel* and *kahal* (see below) are written with the letter *heh*, but *ḥet* and *heh* are similar in both Arabic and Hebrew.
31. *Encyclopedia Judaica*, s.v. Nahman of Bratslav [*sic*]: Teachings, vol. 12, 786.

Na

Naḥ

Naḥma

Naḥman miUman.[32]

His followers are known as *"naḥnaḥim"* after this triangle.

Rabbi Nahman's oral teachings were recorded by his pupil Rabbi Natan Sternharz. Rabbi Natan writes often of haroset in his collection of Rabbi Nahman's sayings. His ideas are based on word plays on the word haroset itself. The Hebrew letters in the word haroset can be rearranged into the words *hass* חס and *root* רות.[33] *Hass* means "have mercy," while *root* is the name of the biblical Ruth, the ancestor of King David and hence of the Messianic line (Ruth 4:13–17). Thus for Rabbi Nahman and his hasidim, haroset is a symbol of God's redemptive mercy in the past, and heralds the future coming of the Messiah.

---

32. This is claimed to be based on a substitution of the four-letter Hebrew name of Nahman for the four-letter name of God. For a discussion of this sort of magical thinking process see J. Trachtenberg, *Jewish Magic and Superstition: A Study in Folk Religion* (New York: Behrman's Jewish Book House, 1939), 78–103.

33. Rabbi Natan Sternhartz, *Seder Haggada shel Pesaḥ: Or Zore'aḥ* (with comments and explanations of Rabbi Nahman of Breslov) (Jerusalem: unknown publisher, 1926), 36–7.

Chapter 5

Modern Haroset: Secularism, Memories and Authenticity

To make *chorissas*: take of almonds or nuts ¼ lb chopped or bruised; scrape the insides of two apples; add 2 ozs of moist sugar, ¼ oz of cinnamon, and two tablespoonfuls of raisin wine. Mix the whole well together and serve...during the first two days of Passover.

Hebrew Cookery by "An Australian Aristologist"

With the dawn of the movement known as the Enlightenment, the influence of religious laws and rabbinic traditions diminished. While the rabbis continued to discuss haroset and give it religious meaning, they now lost their exclusive hold over recorded Jewish memory and the meanings of food. I shall thus be looking at modern writing about haroset in its non-rabbinical cultural contexts: haroset in cookery books on the one hand (such as the Australian one cited above), and in literature on

99

the other. New trends took hold as many religious observances lapsed, but the secular Diaspora still looked back with nostalgia for the lost culture of the religious past. On the other hand, the absence of haroset at the Seder – inadvertent during the Holocaust, but deliberate at the celebrations of the early kibbutzim – led to erasure of Jewish memories.

In this survey of haroset through the ages, I have looked mostly at religious texts, either rabbinical legal works or copies of the traditional Haggada with its commentaries. Indeed, until a few centuries ago, there was very little Jewish writing outside rabbinic literature. At the end of the seventeenth century, however, the Jewish philosopher Baruch Spinoza of Amsterdam challenged traditional Jewish (and Christian) beliefs. He proved to be a harbinger of the Enlightenment movement, which questioned traditional institutions, beliefs, customs and morals. The Jewish community excommunicated Spinoza, but eventually the new questioning penetrated the Jewish communities of Europe. Secular Jewish works began to appear. From this point onwards, haroset appears in novels, essays, memoirs, anthropological analyses – and cookery books. For the first time we find secularized versions of the Haggada. And the development of haroset is now recorded in entirely different ways.

Literary Haroset

Fiction for its own sake, as opposed to moralizing parables, had little or no place in earlier Jewish literature. Once it was established as a new genre, however, it served as fascinating witness to a new Jewish culture, which continued to make use of old traditions.

We have seen how in the border areas of Provence and Italy there was a meeting of Sephardic and Ashkenazic traditions, which produced many variations in the ingredients of haroset found in rabbinic sources. A particularly interesting meeting of these traditions can be seen in nineteenth-century Germany, in a literary, rather than a rabbinic, source. The famous German writer Heinrich Heine wrote several works on Jewish themes, including a fragment of a novel or short story called *The Rabbi of Bachrach* (1824–25). This work includes an account of a Seder set in the Middle Ages in Germany, where the participants are forced to flee from an accusation of ritual murder when the body of a Christian child is discovered, planted under their Seder table. Before this dramatic and gruesome interruption, Heine had described the rabbi's wife bringing the elements of the Seder plate to the table. These include "six little dishes containing symbolical food: an egg, lettuce, horseradish, the bone of a lamb," and "*eine braune Mischung von Rosinen, Zimmet und Nüssen,* a brown mixture of raisins, cinnamon and nuts," which is clearly the rabbi's haroset. The marked absence of apples (or indeed pears) from Ashkenazic haroset seems strange, both in the medieval setting of the story and in Heine's own nineteenth-century Germany. It is, of course, possible that Heine was not interested in the exact ingredients, or that he simply failed to identify them all (his six little dishes, we note, contain only five foods).[1] However, Heine is a writer who shows considerable interest in food, and even wrote a poem in praise of *cholent,* the heavy Jewish Sabbath stew (or as he calls it, *Schalet*).[2] His idea of Heaven, too, is one continual feast, while Hell, in his vision, houses three rows of iron cooking pots – one for boiling Christian sinners, one for Jews and one for infidels. So how can we explain his haroset?

A closer look at nineteenth-century Germany reveals that from the time of the emancipation, German Jews had begun to abandon a large number of the traditions and attitudes of Ashkenazic Judaism, which many of them despised. Some German Jews identified instead with what they saw as the more culturally open, philosophical and aesthetic Sephardic Jewish heritage, deriving from Spain and Portugal. Sephardic models influenced German-Jewish culture in liturgy, synagogue architecture, scholarship and literature.[3] The German-Jewish scholar, philosopher and man of letters, Moses Mendelssohn, made heavy use of Spanish-Jewish sources in the commentary to his German translation of the Torah. The fashionable, so-called "Moorish" synagogue architecture

---

1. Heine was clearly very fond of raisins. In his *Disputation: In der Aula zu Toledo* between Jew and Christian he has his Jewish rabbi tempt the Christian monk with a meal made of the legendary Leviathan served in a heavenly – *himmlisch* – raisin sauce. For a translation (and a recipe for *carpe à la juive* in raisin sauce from Alsace on the French-German border), see J. Nathan, *Quiches, Kugels and Couscous* (New York, 2010), 150–51.
2. See his poem "Prinzessin Sabbath," with a parody of Schiller; and B. Fairley, "Heine and the Festive Board," *University of Toronto Quarterly,* 36 (1967): 209–19.
3. I. Schorsch, *From Text to Context: The Turn to History in Modern Judaism* (Hanover: Brandeis University Press, 1994), 71–92.

also stressed the identification with Spanish models. The synagogue in Oranienbergerstrasse in Berlin is a good example.[4]

Heine, clearly, was among those preoccupied with all things Sephardic. Born into an Ashkenazic family, he laid claim to some Sephardic ancestry. In *The Rabbi of Bachrach,* his fictional rabbi has spent seven years studying in Toledo in Spain, which is perhaps somewhat unlikely for a medieval German rabbinical student. Later in the story, the rabbi meets Don Isaac Abarbanel himself, the Portuguese rabbi, scholar and statesman. So it may well have been the Sephardic connection that led Heine to remove the apples from his haroset (although haroset based mainly on raisins rather than dates is actually more typical of the Spanish Diaspora in Greece and Turkey than of Spain itself). Thus, while Heine's haroset may not be representative of how nineteenth-century German Jews behaved, it did represent in microcosm how some German Jews thought.

A rather different haroset is found in the sensitive short story *Passover,* by contemporary American playwright David Mamet, quoted at the opening of chapters 2 and 3.[5] The story is told in the form of a conversation between a grandmother and a granddaughter, while the child is carefully chopping the ingredients for haroset. Haroset, indeed, is never actually mentioned by name, but it is inferred from the title and the details of the discussion.

The grandmother begins by talking about mortar and bricks with the child, and in their conversation (cited above in the heading to chapter 3), they note how "our sort [of haroset]" is made with apples and raisins, almonds, walnuts, honey, wine and cloves or cinnamon. The illustration on the title page, indeed, is of apples. The raisins and almonds are given their Yiddish name and cultural load: *rozhinkes mit mandelen,* as in the iconic Yiddish song. This Ashkenazic version is carefully distinguished still further from its Sephardic counterpart (quoted

---

4. See the painting by Emil de Cauwer, 1865, on the cover of A. Nachama, J. H. Schoeps and H. Simon, ed., *Jews in Berlin* (Berlin: Henschel, 2002), and R. I. Cohen, "Urban Visibility and Biblical Visions: Jewish Culture in Western and Central Europe in the Modern Age," in *Cultures of the Jews: A New History,* ed. D. Biale (New York: Schocken Books, 2002), 731–96, esp. 745–7.

5. D. Mamet, *Passover* (New York: St Martin's Press, 2002).

in the heading to chapter 2) by noting the figs and dates which make the difference between them. Although the spices here are cut with a knife, the grandmother explains that when she was young, they were pounded with a brass pestle in a mortar, and that "long ago" these implements were of wood.

The knife is then used as a further link to the past and the role it played in another tale of violence against the Jews at Passover. The grandmother tells how her own grandmother saved herself and her family from a pogrom with her knife. She killed the chickens intended for the Seder, scattered their blood around the house and told her family to hide. Thus the villagers who sought to kill this Jewish family thought they had been killed already, and their house was spared. The memories conjured up by the haroset in this story reflect the memories of the original Passover story. They, too, recall both repression and redemption.

Mamet dramatically illustrates the ambiguities of the knife, the potentially dangerous tool that had to kill to save. Indeed, his own treatise on the "nature and purpose of drama," *Three Uses of the Knife*, states that the genuine hero is distinguished by his or her power to resist.[6] Haroset, then, for Mamet, represents the power to resist, and becomes an image for the survival of the Jewish people throughout the generations.

Haroset by Mistake

We have seen how the instructions for making haroset were copied and handed down in rabbinical texts. With time, changes crept in, sometimes intentionally and sometimes unintentionally, including actual mistakes. The situation is not all that different in modern cookery books, which often include recipes that have been copied and adapted from earlier works, sometimes acknowledged, but often not.

An amusing episode of a mistaken haroset has been revealed by Barbara Kirshenblatt-Gimblett.[7] In 1867, a little booklet called *Hebrew*

---

6. D. Mamet, *Three Uses of the Knife: On the Nature and Purpose of Drama* (New York: Vintage Books, 2000).

7. The following account of the mixing up of haroset with *chorissa* is based on Barbara Kirshenblatt-Gimblett's delightful paper: "Hebrew Cookery: An Early Jewish Cookbook from the Antipodes," *Petits propos culinaires* 28 (1988): 11–21.

Cookery was published in Melbourne and London by "an Australian Aristologist" (probably a Tasmanian by the name of Edward Abbott).[8] He wrote that many of his recipes came from *The Jewish Manual*, the first Jewish cookbook published in English, and almost certainly written by Lady Judith Montefiore in London. Lady Judith gives us a valuable record of the cuisine of the more aristocratic Anglo-Jewish community at the end of the nineteenth century. This community was composed primarily of Sephardim originating in Spain and Portugal, like the founders of the Bevis Marks Synagogue mentioned earlier, and like her husband Moses' own family. Their food was strongly influenced by the cuisine of Spain and Portugal.[9]

On one occasion, the Aristologist apparently misunderstood his source. Lady Judith describes, without giving a recipe for, what she calls *chorissa*, "that most refined and savoury of all sausages" which may be procured, she says, at local kosher butchers' shops.[10] However, *chorissa* was not available at all kosher butchers' shops, or perhaps it was sold only by Sephardic butchers. Thus when the Aristologist asked Mr. Barnett, a pastry cook from Melbourne, and Mrs. Isaacs of the London Tavern for the recipe, they clearly thought he meant haroset (pronounced *charoses* by Ashkenazic Jews). And they therefore gave him the recipe for traditional Ashkenazic haroset! He included it in his cookery book:

> To make *chorissas*: take of almonds or nuts ¼ lb chopped or bruised; scrape the insides of two apples; add 2 ozs of moist sugar, ¼ oz of cinnamon, and two tablespoonfuls of raisin wine. Mix the whole well together and serve…during the first two days of Passover.[11]

---

8. "An Australian Aristologist," *Hebrew Cookery* (London/Melbourne: Low & Co./ George Robertson, 1867).
9. A Lady [Judith Cohen Montefiore], ed., *The Jewish Manual or Practical Information in Jewish and Modern Cookery, with a Collection of Valuable Recipes and Hints Relating to the Toilette* (London: T. & W. Boone, 1846; repr. no place: Bibliobazaar, 2006).
10. Montefiore (above, n. 9), 55.
11. Art. cit. (above, n. 7), 12.

This mixture alone would have been perfectly good at the Seder, if rather sweet for some tastes. However, Lady Judith uses *chorissa* as an ingredient in a number of further recipes. Haroset, instead of *chorissa*, may in fact have worked in recipes such as fowl stewed with rice and *chorissa*,[12] but *chorissa* omelette (finely minced *chorissa* added to eggs) and "Palestine soup" (a meat and vegetable broth made with *chorissa* and Jerusalem artichokes)[13] present quite another story. One wonders if anyone (including the author) ever tried out his recipes.

Nostalgic Haroset

With the advancing of modernity and the continuing spread of Jewish communities throughout the Diaspora, accounts of haroset relate more and more to individual experiences. Secular literature begins to reflect nostalgia for the lost experience of the traditional Seder, where the authors had incorporated the taste of their childhood.

"Seder at Grandpa's," by Marghanita Laski, found in the *Passover Anthology*, is an example of a new genre of memoirs,[14] in which the Seder held in memory of the Exodus has become a memory itself. Laski was the granddaughter of Moses Gaster, the Ḥakham[15] of Bevis Marks Synagogue, but she herself was an avowed atheist. Laski's description of the Seder is sardonically amusing and detached. This may not be surprising in a secular Oxford-educated intellectual who is fully assimilated into English culture, and for whom religion – and haroset – may be relegated to childish memories.

But not all modern writers wished to relegate their childhood memories to a faded past. Often, they pined for their youth, when the community was intact and the identity expressed in the foods of the Seder was unequivocal. Farideh Goldin, a displaced Iranian Jewish

---

12. Art. cit. (above, n. 7), 16.
13. Montefiore (above, n. 9): *chorissa* omelette: 79; Palestine soup: 23. "Jerusalem" artichokes, of course, have nothing to do with the city; they are related to the sunflower, *girasole* in Italian: see on this: A. Davidson, *The Oxford Companion to Food* (Oxford/New York: Oxford University Press, 1999, 2nd edition).
14. M. Laski, "Seder at Grandpa's," in *The Passover Anthology*, ed. P. Goodman (Philadelphia: Jewish Publication Society of America, 1973).
15. Ḥakham is the title given to the local rabbi in Sephardic communities.

woman who wrote about her experiences, has presented haroset as the subject of nostalgic longing for an irrevocable past. Goldin writes evocatively of how she repeatedly tried and failed to make haroset that would recapture the taste of her childhood. Finally, her father came from Iran to join her in America, with the missing ingredient, his own homemade wine vinegar. When he opened the bottle, she writes, the house was filled with "the aroma of Passovers past, of a home lost, of a community in disarray."[16] Like the communities in exile described by the sociologist David Sutton in *Remembrance of Repasts*, Goldin has expressed her nostalgia for her home, typically remembering it through its iconic foods.

Memory and Erasure: Haroset and the Holocaust

In the introduction to this chapter I noted that haroset is absent from accounts of the Seder during the Holocaust, and from the few surviving Holocaust Haggadas, although there are moving testimonies about the importance that the performance of the Passover Seder took on under Nazi rule.[17] Even in times of extreme food shortages, the commonplace ingredients of matza – flour and water – were usually available. Thus people could and did bake matza, even in Nazi-occupied territories, albeit in fear of their lives. Substitutes were found for wine: raisins were soaked to make raisin wine, or beetroot colored the water red. By celebrating the Seder and eating or simply remembering eating its symbolic foods, Jews were proclaiming their identity as Jews. In particular, like their forefathers in Egypt and the rabbis of Yavne, they were expressing their identity as free men and women, however oppressive the outside world. They were creating hope of eventual redemption. But haroset, with its expensive and exotic ingredients, was difficult to obtain. Moreover, as we know, it is not mentioned in the biblical story of the redemption from Egypt. It is not surprising, then, that it completely disappeared from the record. Presumably, this omission was compelled by the terrible circumstances.

---

16. Farideh Goldin, "My Father's *Kharoset*," *Jewish Quarterly* 205 (2007): 88.
17. I. Levin, ed., *Dam VaEsh VeTimrot Ashan: Haggadat HaShoah LaPesaḥ* (Tel Aviv: Yediot Aḥaronot, 2008); H. Strauss, "Passover in the Ghettoes of the 'General Government,'" *Massuah Annual* 8 (1980 [Hebrew]): 83–102.

New Haggadas for New Jews: Haroset and the Kibbutz

It is not so immediately obvious, however, why haroset would be absent
from the Passover celebrations of the early kibbutzim in Palestine. The
members of the early kibbutzim came to the Land of Israel in order to
create a new society, deliberately cutting themselves off from the traditional Judaism of Europe. They intended to base themselves on the
Tanakh, the Hebrew Bible, and return to the "true roots" of the Jewish
people in their own land. As part of this ethos, they created for themselves new ways of celebrating the traditional Jewish festivals, including
Passover, and they re-created their own form of Haggada. Many of their
Haggadas, song sheets, programs and leaflets containing reflections on
Passover have been preserved in the Kibbutz Festivals Archive in Kibbutz Beit HaShitta. Here, for example, I found the account of Zeev
Wachskortz, who wrote in 1922 that Passover for him was a festival of
"dead historical memories." He was angry that the members of his kibbutz, Deganya Gimmel, had celebrated that year in the same way as
"our fathers in Berditchev and Tarnow." Identifying himself as one of
the "*apikorsim* (apostates)," and apparently reflecting the views of many
contemporaries, he claimed that this sort of celebration was meaning-
less, saying, "We must create our own festivals, not necessarily on the
day we left Egypt."

Thus the kibbutzim began to celebrate Passover in new and different ways, using the Haggada and traditional biblical texts as points
of departure. For them, Passover represented a spring harvest festival,
often with quotations from the Song of Songs, as well as a memorial to
the Exodus from Egypt. After all, the kibbutz members had come from
the Diaspora to the Land of Israel. Thus kibbutz Haggadas gave new
symbolic meaning to the Four Cups of wine: these represented Spring,
the Exodus from Egypt, *Kibbutz Galuyot* (the Ingathering of the Exiles)
and Redemption (or alternatively, the Blessing of the Land).

The daily experiences of working the land were also included,
often in the words of passages from the prophets about harvest and
fruitfulness. Amos, the proto-socialist prophet, is particularly popular. The 1947 Haggada of HaShomer HaTza'ir includes the following,
edited verses (omitting the next words in the biblical verse: "says the
Lord"):

> "Behold, the days come...
> When the ploughman shall overtake the reaper,
> And the treader of grapes him who sows seed;
> And the mountains shall drop sweet wine,
> And all the hills shall melt.
> And I will bring back the captivity of My people of Israel,
> And they shall build the waste cities and inhabit them;
> And they shall plant vineyards, and drink their wine,
> They shall also make gardens, and eat the fruit of them." (Amos
> 9:13–15)

But life was not all bountiful harvests. And kibbutz Haggadas from the late 1930s and the 1940s were also written in the shadow of the Holocaust. Many contain angry and violent passages and illustrations that draw parallels between the Egyptian slavery and the European concentration camps. The Haggada from Kibbutz Beit Alfa, published in 1945, for example, begins with *nekama*, revenge, written big three times on the first page. Other Haggadas, however, are more hopeful. Another Haggada from the same year from Kibbutz Eyal states that on "other nights we sat in the Diaspora, in ghettos and camps. Tonight we recline in our home." Many kibbutz Haggadas from this time cite the verses from Jeremiah (31:15) we noted in chapter 3 about Rachel weeping for her children and refusing to be comforted, which have resonated with Jews through the ages. But they then add to this sad picture the continuation of the passage (31:16–17) with its prophecy of comfort, foretelling the return of Israel to its own land:

> Keep thy voice from weeping...
> For thy work shall be rewarded...
> And there is hope for thy future...
> And thy children shall come back again to their own border.[18]

On many kibbutzim these verses were sung, with a soloist singing of Rachel weeping, and the community responding with the prophecy of comfort.

---

18. The repeated refrain "thus says the Lord" is omitted from the kibbutz versions.

Many of the kibbutz Haggadas do not even mention the meal – the kibbutz antagonism to old European Jewish traditions appears to have included deprecating the traditional stress on food, which they objected to on principle. Although matza and the Four Cups of wine remained as part of the Seder ritual, in many cases the Seder plate disappeared. One kibbutz Passover leaflet from the 1990s includes a memoir of Passovers past that recalls music, sights and smells, but not tastes. And the smells recalled are of animals, machines, dusty fields, "the hot perfume of ripe grain," and new clothes from the communal store, but not of food, or even wine.[19]

Together with the Seder plate and its other symbolic foods, haroset, too, disappeared from almost all kibbutz Seders. It belonged to the rejected past. Its spices represented expensive and unnecessary luxury. By 1987, it became historicized, the subject of a note in a pre-Passover leaflet edited by Avraham Aderet and distributed as an adult education resource by Kibbutz Ayelet HaShahar. This leaflet quotes material from talmudic and later rabbinic sources to explain the symbolism of haroset, and cites a combination of Ashkenazic apples and Sephardic dates, with nuts, spices and wine. Surprisingly, perhaps, it also quotes Rabbi Nahman of Breslov. But this is not the Rabbi Nahman we saw above with a messianic interpretation of haroset. Aderet finds another play on words by Rabbi Nahman which would have meant much more to his audience. He marks the difference between *avoda* (labor) in the Land of Israel, which produces the fruits from which haroset is made, and *avdut* (slavery) in Egypt, which was centered around the clay which haroset symbolizes. In the 1980s the kibbutz movement was, of course, still committed to the ethos of *avoda* as labor on the land, and this symbolism for haroset would still have been meaningful. But haroset itself for the kibbutz members was now part of written history, not the living present.

The one exception to the above developments was the small group of religious kibbutzim, where the communal Seder was a highlight of the Jewish calendar, before privatization transferred the yearly

---

19. M. Tamir, "Memories of the Sounds, Sights and Smells of Passover," *Kibbutz Afikim Passover Leaflet* (Kibbutz Afikim: self-published, 1997 [Hebrew]).

ritual to individual homes. Sarah Levi, a teacher, who arrived in Palestine from Hungary in the years around the Second World War, was one of the founding members of Kibbutz Saad. She made it her special task to prepare haroset for the several hundred people on the kibbutz, each year. It took her and a team of helpers three days' hard work. Sarah died recently, but her recipe, hand-written on an ageing scrap of paper, has survived:

<u>Passover 1983</u>

<u>*Haroset*</u>

Apples	— 2 full black containers
Bananas	— 1 almost full black container
Dates	— 12 kilos
Nuts	— 15 kilos
Liqueur/alcohol	— 13 bottles
Wine	— 22 — (11 red 11 white)
Sugar	— 1 kilo
Cinnamon	— ½ kilo

Preparationmethod	— nuts	— grate on medium grater
	apples	— *ditto*
	dates	— half the quantity with 5 bottles of wine in the *stefan*
	bananas	— in the *stefan*

The *stefan* was an immense grinding machine, usually used for meat. This recipe is firmly rooted in the later Ashkenazic tradition, apart from the addition of bananas, typical of modern Israel, and the rather large amount of alcohol.

THE MODERN SEDER TABLE

Geography, Culture and Haroset

Overall, looking at the different sorts of modern haroset in Jewish Diaspora communities, it is clear that there is a geographical distribution. Apple-based haroset is used by Ashkenazic communities, now including much of North America. Date-based haroset is used by most Sephardic or Mizrahi communities, including Jews originally from Iraq, Iran, North Africa and Yemen, as well as Spain and Portugal. The Iraqis, and the Iraqi Diaspora communities in India, make almost the same haroset as Rav Saadia Gaon in the tenth century, although they leave out the vinegar. Other Sephardic communities have their own particular additions; Persians, for example, use pomegranates. In the transitional area of the Balkans, in Greece and Turkey, haroset is often raisin-based – using black raisins. These practices are clearly related to the availability of the fruits. Dates do not grow in Ashkenaz.

But the influence of textual sources is also still a factor. As we have seen, the eleventh-century inclusion of fruits mentioned in the Song of Songs, or other fruits that symbolize the Jewish people, opened the way for variations. Ironically, although this came from the Sephardic *Teshuvot HaGeonim*, it was the Ashkenazic Tosafists who preserved this tradition in their texts.

There is, however, another haroset custom, which was first noted in Ashkenaz, and is now, as my modern informants tell me, only preserved among Sephardim. We saw that the Jerusalem Talmud says that haroset is in in memory of clay or blood, and reports rabbis differing as to whether it should be made thick or more runny. In medieval Ashkenaz, this debate was resolved by the Tosafist Rabbi Yehiel, who said it should be made thick at first, and thinned down with wine or vinegar at the Seder table. I found no Ashkenazim, however, who make their haroset this way today. Perhaps the experience of blood libels in Ashkenaz meant that no one wanted to preserve a memory of blood. We saw earlier how the *Taz*, who lived through pogroms in Poland, says that red wine should not be used at all at the Seder. My Ashkenazic acquaintances do put red wine in their haroset, but they add it before the Seder, in the kitchen.

Some community customs were lost through marriages between people from different Jewish communities. Perhaps both parents' traditional haroset would appear on the Seder table for a generation, but the children would not preserve both traditions. However, sometimes one particular ingredient would be kept through the ages, a taste memory of the past. Estelle Asher comes from a family of Spanish Jews who were expelled in 1492 and fled to Amsterdam. Later they moved to England, where Estelle's father, Benjamin Montanjees, married Vera Perlman, who was of Polish origin, in the old Sephardic Bevis Marks Synagogue, before immigrating to New Zealand. Estelle now lives in Israel. When I asked her what she puts in her haroset, she listed the ingredients of a typical Ashkenazic haroset, with one exception. "Of course, we always use hazelnuts," she said. Standard, contemporary, Ashkenazic haroset contains walnuts and almonds, but not hazelnuts. But, as we saw, hazelnuts were used by the Italian Rabbi Ovadiah from Bertinoro in the sixteenth century, in the *Arosset* prescribed in Italy for Spanish Jews in 1656, as well as in the Sephardic haroset recipe discovered in the Bevis Marks Synagogue archives from 1726. Estelle's hazelnuts have traveled through history all over the world.

The make-up of haroset is partly a function of what is prescribed in the standard rabbinical texts, but it is also influenced by the local social and geographical context. Culture, as we saw in the "sephardizing" haroset of the German writer Heine and the American post-Holocaust interpretation of haroset by David Mamet, strongly influenced the development of haroset. Haggadas have always reflected the culture in which they were created. The best-known American Haggada, the *Maxwell House Haggada*, was produced in the USA as an advertisement for coffee. In present-day Israel, it is quite common for different social groups, for example kibbutzim or commercial organizations such as banks, to produce their own Haggadas. Many of these have the standard text with, at most, some new illustrations, but others have attempted to write new texts, in an attempt to be "more relevant" to modern Israeli audiences. Not all the effects may be intentional. Thus an undated Israeli Haggada produced by Rabbi M. Avital for Kupat Ḥolim Klallit, Israel's leading Sick Fund, includes instructions for preparing haroset that sound like a pharmacist's instructions for preparing a medication: "You can make it yourself or buy it. Empty the package, soften it with a little wine and it can then be used for dipping the bitter herbs in the haroset."[20]

---

20. M. Avital, *Haggada shel Pesaḥ shel Kupat Ḥolim* (Merkaz Kupat Ḥolim: no place, no date: acquired by Tel Aviv University Library in 1971), no page numbers.

Haroset in a Changing Society

Men in the kitchen

In talking to people about haroset, I found that it is often made by men, in both Ashkenazic and Sephardic communities. This raises a question since, in traditional societies, kitchen and food might be expected to be the exclusive domain of women.

I can suggest a number of reasons for this. First, there is a question, dating back to the Mishna, as to whether haroset is a mitzva.[21] This doubt is not completely resolved in the sources. In the common sexist attitudes that were entrenched in Jewish culture (as in many others) in earlier times, and which unfortunately persist in parts to this day, the following rationale may have been employed: if haroset really is a mitzva, then it becomes important, and therefore something not beneath a man's dignity to prepare, even something too important to leave to "mere" women. One modern rabbinic text I read even says that simply laying out the Seder table may be too important to be left to women.[22]

On the other hand, some women I interviewed reported that the method their community used to prepare haroset was considered such heavy work that the men had to do it. Squeezing soaked dates through cheesecloth and wringing them out, as reported by Jews from India, was a case in point.

A third explanation of why the task of preparing haroset was assigned to men might be that it was perceived to be an unskilled task. Passover cookery, and especially baking, requires much skill and creativity, since many familiar ingredients are forbidden and must be replaced. It would therefore generally have been seen by gender-segregated societies of the time as a woman's task, since women were seen as presiding over the kitchen.[23] Making haroset, on the other hand – or at least uncooked Ashkenazic haroset – is one of the few unskilled tasks, and could thus safely be left to men.

A last possible explanation relates to marriages between Jews from different traditions and communities. An Ashkenazic man might

---

21. We saw the Rambam's approach in chapter 2.
22. M. Y. Weingarten (no relation), *HaSeder HeArukh*, vol. I (Jerusalem: M. Y. Weingarten, 1993), 108–9 and bibliography there.
23. In parallel to the rabbinical text above, a task too important to leave to men!

rt*

prefer the haroset his family had made to that of his wife's Sephardic community – in which case she might well tell him to make it himself!

We have seen, perhaps surprisingly, that in the traditionally conservative Yemenite community it is common for husband and wife to make haroset together. This practice presumably stems from the Yemenite interpretation of the passage from the Jerusalem Talmud that, as noted in chapter 1, refers to haroset under the same name as the Yemenite Jews call it, *dukkeh*, and can be interpreted to read, "She grinds it with him." This, indeed, is how the authoritative Yemenite Rabbi Yosef Kappah reads it in his edition of the Haggada.[24]

Feminist haroset on the Seder plate

As one of the symbolic foods of the Seder, haroset is placed on the Seder plate, together with the egg, salt water, *zero'a* (shank bone), *karpas* (green herbs or potato) and *maror* (bitter herbs), usually on top of the three matzas. Feminists have recently taken to adding an orange to these six standard elements, a practice explained by a modern urban legend.[25] One version tells of a group of women who asked their local Orthodox rabbi if they may lead the community prayers. The rabbi was horrified. A woman leading the prayers in the synagogue, he exclaimed, would be as out of place as an orange on the Seder plate! In response, some women have begun placing an orange on their Seder plates, to signify their objection to this sort of attitude.

But it is not necessary to break so openly with tradition to reinterpret the Seder plate from a feminist perspective. Ruth Fredman Cernea has written an interesting anthropological analysis of the Passover Seder, and its symbols on the plate.[26] She relates to Ashkenazic practice, using the plate layout outlined by the Ari:

---

24. Y. Kappah, ed., *Sefer Agaddeta DePisḥa* (Jerusalem: HaAguda LeHatzalat Ginzei Teiman, with Mosad HaRav Kook, 1958).

25. Analysis of the group of legends around the orange: S. Zylberberg, "Oranges and Seders: Symbols of Jewish Women's Wrestlings," *Nashim* 5 (2002): 148–71.

26. R. Fredman Cernea, *The Passover Seder: An Anthropological Perspective on Jewish Culture* (Lanham: University Press of America, 1995), originally published as R. Fredman Gruber, *The Passover Seder: Afikoman in Exile* (Philadelphia: University of Pennsylvania Press, 1981).

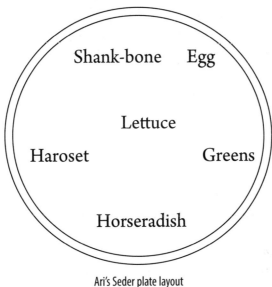

Shank-bone   Egg

Lettuce

Haroset   Greens

Horseradish

Ari's Seder plate layout

Cernea looks at the significance of directions in Jewish culture and concludes that "up" and "right" are privileged over "down" and "left." The
shank bone – hard, white, dry and associated with meat – is interpreted
by her as male. Haroset – sweet and wet, containing red wine associated
with blood and raw fruits associated with fertility – is situated below it,
and seen as female. The position of the haroset – "right" but "down" –
shows the "compromised" position of woman, and her association with
life and death.

Cernea's interpretation is doubtful, given other authoritative traditional patterns of setting out the symbolic foods on the
plate. Rabbi Elijah of Vilna, the Vilna Gaon, places the shank bone
below the haroset.[27] And the impossibility of seeing Rabbi Elijah
as a proto-feminist should lead us to cast some doubt on Cernea's
interpretation.[28]

---

27. Rabbi Elijah ben Solomon Zalman of Vilna, commonly known as the Vilna Gaon or
    HaGra (=HaGaon Rabbi Elijah) (1720–1797), *Seder Haggada shel Pesah*, ed. N Pfeffer
    (New York: Makhon HaGra, 1999).
28. The Vilna Gaon even advised women not to go to synagogue: A. Weiss, *Women at*

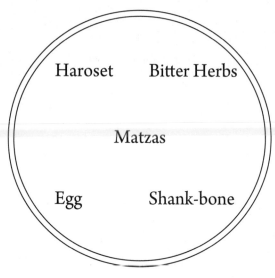

Vilna Gaon's Seder plate layout

Child's play at the Seder table

The Haggada, from its inception, has always been child-centered. Its very name, Haggada, a tale or a narrative, is taken from the biblical verse "And thou shalt tell it (*vehiggadeta*) to thy son" (Ex. 13:8). The narrative begins as a reply to the youngest child's question, "Why is this night different from all other nights?" (*Ma Nishtana* ...). As any good educator knows, the child's attention can be kept by various different strategies. At the Seder these include games with words, and even food and drink, such as spilling a drop of wine for each of the Ten Plagues, and playing on salt and bitter and sour and sweet, as tiny tantalizing tastes of food succeed each other before the meal. Indeed, the Babylonian Talmud (Pesaḥim 116a) specifies that one reason for dipping the bitter herbs into the haroset, the second dipping at the Seder, is to encourage the child to ask.

We have seen some of the verbal and visual games that developed over the years. By the modern period, some of these were explicitly aimed

---

Prayer: A Halakhic Analysis of Women's Prayer Groups (Hoboken, NJ: Ktav, 1990), 44.

at children. The ingredients in haroset, for example, are taught in this ditty from a mid-twentieth-century American Jewish children's book:

> Apples, raisins
> Chopped up fine
> Cinnamon, nuts
> And sweet red wine.[29]

In true Seder tradition, these rhyming verses make learning easier and more palatable for the child.

Seder traditions also include a more tangible plaything, not originally intended for children, but certainly taken up by them: the haroset wheelbarrow. In their discussions of observing the commandments, the rabbis of the Talmud introduced the concept of *hiddur mitzva* – beautifying the mitzva.[30] They ruled that it was desirable to go further than the mere observance of a mitzva. Thus ritual objects should be made of the most beautiful and expensive materials a Jew could afford, to show how much importance she or he gave to doing God's will. For example, it is good enough to light the Sabbath candles in lamps made of pottery, wood or iron, but lighting them in silver or gold lamps or candlesticks would "beautify" the mitzva. Passover was no exception. The beautiful illuminated Haggadas, which we looked at in chapter 2, were presumably commissioned by owners who had this tradition in mind.

Similarly, the Seder plate was often made of decorated porcelain or silver, with sets of little bowls or plates for the ritual foods, including the haroset. In Europe, tiny silver wheelbarrows were designed especially for haroset, as a tangible reminder of working the clay used to make bricks for building the cities of Egypt. This delightful conceit is, of course, anachronistic. The wheelbarrow was probably invented by the Greeks, although credit is usually given to the Chinese in the third century CE. It certainly was not in use when the Children of Israel were

---

29. S. R. Weilerstein, *What the Moon Brought* (Philadelphia: Jewish Publication Society, 1942).
30. Makhon HaEntziklopedya HaTalmudit, *Entziklopedya Talmudit* (Jerusalem: Yad HaRav Hertzog, 1957), vol. 8, s.v. *hiddur mitzva*.

Haroset wheelbarrow

slaves in Egypt. Nevertheless, what began as a way to further beautify the mitzva of haroset soon became a way to arouse the curiosity and interest of the children. Aharon Oppenheimer, Professor of Jewish History at Tel Aviv University, was born in Tel Aviv to a family from Germany. He told me that as a small child he had far fewer toys than children today, so he was endlessly fascinated by the tiny gleaming haroset wheelbarrow. It had a wheel that actually turned, and he would play with it all through the Seder.

Most of the haroset wheelbarrows I have seen are tiny, and would not hold enough to feed a big family. But the wheelbarrows seem to have come mostly from Germany, where the custom was merely to dip into the haroset, and not to eat it. So maybe it held enough haroset for those families who simply used haroset for dipping, and did not actually eat it!

Authenticity and Innovation

Today there are many innovations in haroset recipes, in keeping with the present trend in foodways to always look for the new and exciting, rather than keep to old traditions. Some of the older traditions, of course, were innovations in their day, which were not approved by the rabbis of the time.

Such was the case with the ground potsherds or grit, fiercely opposed by the Hida in the eighteenth century. But ground potsherds are still being used in the Sephardic tradition. Menahem Pariente, who was born in Lisbon to a family who comes from Gibraltar, and now lives in Israel, brought me a Hebrew and Spanish Haggada printed in London in 1813, where the ingredients for haroset include the "dust of bricks ground very fine."[31] He

Preparing brick dust at the Pariente home

---

31. Jacob Meldula de Amsterdam, ed., *Orden de la Agada de Pesah, en Hebraico y Español, segun uzan los Judios, Españoles, y Portuguezes, traducido del Hebraico y Caldeo* (London: L. Alexander, 1813).

Adding brick dust to the Parientes' haroset

told me his family follows these instructions for their haroset, and that they always boil their potsherd before grinding it up.

Because Ashkenazic haroset is almost always the same, and also because it is the most common in the United States, there is a possibility that it will eventually become the dominant haroset. A fellow reader in the university library whose family came from Iraq told me: "We don't have proper haroset – only dates and a few nuts." For her, "proper haroset" was Ashkenazic haroset, and she was amazed and pleased to find that hers was in fact the authentic haroset of Rav Saadia Gaon from Babylonia, or modern Iraq (but without the vinegar). Some families, of course, are giving up on making their own haroset. A combined "Ashkephardic" version with both apples and dates is on sale in jars in the supermarket, and it is this haroset that is distributed to the needy. On the other hand, there is also a threat from excessive innovations – I can only see the faintest whiff of authenticity in "Golden Mango haroset,"[32]

---

32. Mangoes do not seem to have reached the Middle East before the twentieth century. See on this: S. G. Harrison, G. B. Masefield, M. Wallis, *The Oxford Book of Food Plants* (London: Peerage Books, 1985).

one of the many haroset recipes to be found today on the internet, not to mention Ben & Jerry's haroset-flavored ice-cream.[33]

But as in the Middle Ages, Jews are still adding locally available ingredients to their haroset, hoping these will, again, be approved retrospectively by the rabbis. We have noted that bananas are popular as an ingredient of haroset in Israel. They have been known in the country at least since the Middle Ages, when the Crusaders called them "fruit of paradise," but I am not aware of any haroset recipes using bananas before modern times.[34] I was told by several people about a revealing attempt to authenticize their use: bananas go black, which makes the haroset look more like mud or clay.

I have come across one innovation which innovates precisely because it is trying to be ultra-authentic. We have seen how the rabbis who discuss apples in haroset consistently say that these were included in haroset to make it acidic, "*lekahoyei*," an Aramaic word which means literally "to set the teeth on edge." In pre-modern times, as noted in chapter 1, most apples were sourer than our apples, which are bred to be sweet, particularly in the United States. A recent internet discussion of haroset by an American rabbi, Howard (Chaim) Jachter, protests that the Talmud could not possibly have meant the apples we are familiar with when it wrote that haroset must be acidic in memory of *tapuah*, the apple. He resolves this problem with a quotation from Rav Joseph Dov Soloveitchik, the foremost American Modern Orthodox authority, known as the Rav. Rav Soloveitchik cites a different text, not related to haroset, where the word *tapuah* is interpreted by the Tosafists not as apple, but as citron (etrog), the fragrant, acidic fruit used on the festival of Sukkot.[35] So Rabbi Jachter includes etrog, rather than apple, in his haroset, an innovation in the

---

33. https://www.huffingtonpost.com/2015/04/01/charoset-ben-and-jerrys-is-the-real-deal_n_6977854.html (accessed April 2018).

34. The first report of bananas in Europe comes from Theophrastus (c. 370–287 BCE) in his *History of Plants*, which used reports sent back by Alexander the Great's expedition, detailing plants from Persia, India and Afghanistan. See on this: A. Dalby, *Food in the Ancient World from A to Z* (London: Routledge, 2003), s.v. Theophrastus.

35. Tosafot on Taanit 29b.

name of authenticity.[36] It is unclear to me, however, whether Rabbi Jachter actually eats this haroset, for he concludes his discussion with a mention of the German custom of dipping the bitter herbs in the haroset and then shaking it off, without eating the haroset at all.

---

36. H. Jachter, "The Mitzvah of Charoset": https://www.koltorah.org/halachah/the-mitzvah-of-charoset-by-rabbi-chaim-jachter (accessed April 2018), quoting J. D. Soloveitchik, *Nefesh HaRav*, ed. T. Shechter (Jerusalem: Reishit Yerushalayim), 209–10. The identification of the apples in haroset with etrogs was discussed at length by Rabbi Hanokh ben Joseph David Teitelbaum (1884–1943), of Satmar, in his *Responsa Yad Ḥanokh* 8 (accessed from the Bar Ilan Responsa project). The *Yad Ḥanokh* even suggests that the letter *aleph* ("a" or "e") in the Ari's haroset *ev"en* might have referred to an etrog, rather than to an *apfel*. However, he says that since the Jewish women in Egypt gave birth under the apple trees, there would have been more space for childbirth under a real apple tree rather than under an etrog tree!

Chapter 6

My Grandmother's Haroset: Recipes from Around the Jewish World

There seems to be no end to modern recipes for haroset. Ingredients vary from country to country – sometimes from region to region – and even from family to family. There is general reverence for tradition on the one hand – some informants quoted passages from the Talmud almost verbatim, clearly handed down orally – while on the other, it is clear that compromises have been made to accommodate different taste preferences inside and outside the family.

I interviewed a series of people from different backgrounds in Israel and elsewhere to find out how they made their haroset. Most of their recipes do not indicate quantities. The makers work by sight and taste, and estimate quantities according to the number of people they expect at their Seder, just as I do. They use a variety of methods to prepare haroset. The traditional pestle and mortar are now used by very few, although I personally still find these by far the best tools for breaking up walnuts. Some use other outdated technologies, like the hand-operated meat grinder to crush nuts, perhaps because of a feeling that somehow this is closer to old traditions or perhaps simply because they have no way of making their electric blender kosher for Passover.

I present these recipes precisely as my informants gave them, arranged more or less geographically.

HAROSET FROM ENGLAND

Cecilia Pomerantz's Ashkenazic Haroset

The recipe for my own haroset was passed down by my mother Esther Shannon, who inherited it from her mother Cecilia Pomerantz, née Herscovici. At the turn of the twentieth century, my grandmother moved from *Rumania* to *London*, where she married my grandfather, who came from *Russia*. My grandmother's haroset was the standard Ashkenazic version.

Weingarten family archive

My grandmother, Cecilia Pomerantz

My mother grated her apples on a coarse hand-grater. She chopped the nuts in a wooden bowl with a mezzaluna chopper, as well as raisins if she could get them – raisins were not always available with a "Kosher for Passover" label in post-war England. As noted in chapter 3, the fifteenth-century *Leket Yosher* had banned the use of dried figs or raisins on Passover for fear they may have been dried with flour. Depending on the type of apples I use, this haroset is not always sweet enough for my family, so I add sugar to taste. If the mixture is too wet, I add some of the grated coconut, always on hand in my kitchen at Passover.

> 6 grated apples
> A handful of almonds
> A handful of walnuts
> Cinnamon powder
> Sweet red wine
>
> Optional:
> Raisins
> A little sugar
> Desiccated coconut

Val Mars' Haroset from London

Val Mars is a food historian from *London*. Her recipe for haroset came from her mother who belonged to the Sephardic Montefiore family. They lived in *England* but were originally from *Italy*. Her mother was the daughter of the Alice Lucas who translated Hebrew poetry into English.

> 2 oz stoneless raisins
> 1 apple
> 2 oz cinnamon
> Ground biscuit
> 1 banana (optional)

The mixture is made into balls, which are rolled in the cinnamon.

HAROSET FROM ITALY

Bianca Zan's Haroset from the Border Lands

Bianca Zan née Rocca comes from *Ancona* in *Italy*. She learned the recipe for her haroset from her grandmother, who was supervisor of the community's matza baking. She had spent some time in Austria, so Bianca is unsure whether her haroset was Italian or Austrian. However, her family, whose name was Rossi, had been in Italy for two thousand years. They were related to the Italian Jewish composer Salamone di Rossi. They believed the name Rossi (red) signified their origin in Maaleh Adumim (literally "Red Ascent"), between Jerusalem and Jericho.

> Raisins
> Prunes
> Dates
> Apples
> Orange juice
> Sweet red wine

Cook in a pan for a short time until it is the consistency of jam – to resemble clay. Add crushed pecans, in memory of grit. (Adding grit to haroset is first mentioned by the *Shibbolei HaLeket* from thirteenth-century Rome.)

HAROSET FROM GIBRALTAR

Menahem Pariente's Spanish and Portuguese Haroset

Menahem Pariente's family have a tradition that they came from *Asturias* (today part of *Spain*). The name Pariente means relative, because they are related to the royal House of David. After the Jews were expelled from Spain in 1492, they moved to *North Africa* and then *Gibraltar*. Menahem himself was born in *Lisbon*. His mother's family, the Benadys, also lived in *Morocco* and *Gibraltar*. Both families made almost the same haroset. The Parientes are proud of their unusual custom of adding ground potsherd to their haroset, the Hida's strenuous objections notwithstanding. (There is a picture of Menahem adding ground potsherd to his haroset at the end of chapter 5.) "According to my late mother," said Menahem, "the custom

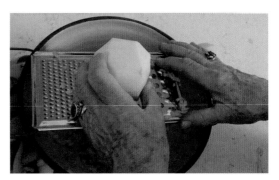

Almonds

Wine

Mix

Photographs: Bruria Pasternak

of her family in Gibraltar was to add a large quantity of vinegar to the haroset to make it liquid. To my mind, this defeats the purpose of having the children involved in the Seder, as this haroset with vinegar tasted quite awful. Luckily for us, my father's family used a small quantity of dry wine just to make the haroset spreadable." The Parientes are the only family I met who still knew about the custom of using vinegar in haroset.

> Nuts
> Almonds
> Apples
> Bananas
> Cinnamon
> Sugar
> A little ground potsherd
> Dry wine or vinegar

Cook all the ingredients together.

HAROSET FROM GREECE

Sophie Matsa's Balkan Haroset

Sophie Matsa née Negrin told me that her family came from *Trikkela* near *Larissa* in *Greece* where there was an old Jewish community, which they say dated back to the fourth century. Her father was a hat maker, which was a traditional trade among Greek Jews. During the Second World War, her father heard what had happened to the Jews of Athens and Salonica and took all his family to hide in the mountains. Her haroset is traditional among Greek Jews. Sophie gave me quantities for eight people, which she said were approximate and could be altered according to taste.

> ¼ kilo seedless white raisins (in Greece there were no seedless raisins, so they used the black ones with seeds)
> ¼ kilo walnuts
> Juice of 1 orange
> 1 apple

A little sugar
1 tablespoon of wine ("I use sweet wine")
2 tablespoons of matza meal

Optional:
Bananas
Dates

The raisins are soaked for several hours, then ground with the rest of the ingredients.

HAROSET FROM TURKEY

Ruti Israel's Balkan Haroset from Istanbul

Ruti Israel's haroset comes from her mother-in-law, who is from *Istanbul*, in *Turkey*.

Black muscatel raisins with stones
Wine

Grind the raisins together with their stones to make a thick black paste. Add wine to soften it. The haroset should be black like clay.

Vicki Nakar's Balkan Haroset from Izmir (Smyrna)

Pitted (stoned) dates
Grated apples
Raisins
Crushed nuts

Optional:
A little wine
A little cinnamon

Crush the dates then add the apples, and cook with a little water until soft. Then add the raisins and nuts.

HAROSET FROM GEORGIA

Natella Hahiashvili's Border Land Haroset

Natella Hahiashvili from *Oni* in *Georgia* told me her haroset is "like that of all Georgian Jews." She uses "all the fruits that are available or in season." Pomegranates, for example, are not in season, but as we will see from Esther Berukhin's Persian haroset below, they would be stored from the previous autumn. Natella's haroset was one of the few modern ones I found that uses pears. (Pears were traditionally used in haroset in Germany in the Middle Ages, as we saw in chapter 3.)

> Walnuts
> Hazelnuts
> Almonds
> Apples
> Pears
> Bananas
> Pomegranates
> Quinces
> Raisins
> Sugar
> Honey
> Sweet red wine
> Matza meal
>
> Optional:
> Dates

Grind the nuts and fruit separately, then mix with ground raisins, together with dates, if you like. Add sugar, honey, wine and enough matza meal to make a stiff paste.

HAROSET FROM THE "STANS"

Zippora Shaharabani's Haroset from Bokhara or Afganistan

Zippora Shaharabani's haroset comes from her mother Hanna Mashiah, who came from a *Bokharan* family that moved to *Balh, Afghanistan.*

Zippora does not know if her haroset is Bokharan or Afghan. "My mother," she said, "would wash, dry and grind the dates, but today I buy a ready paste."

> Walnuts
> Almonds
> Dates
> Sweet red wine

Grind the nuts, then mix with date paste. The day before Passover, mix this with the wine until the texture is like jam.

Zoya Leviva's Haroset from Uzbekistan

Zoya Leviva comes from *Samarkand*, in present-day *Uzbekistan*, not far from *Bokhara*. When I met her, she was visiting her Israeli family, who speak four languages at home: Persian, Bokharan, Russian and Hebrew. Since she now lives in New York, she speaks English as well.

> Black raisins
> Almonds
> Red wine, sweet or dry
> Optional:
> Walnuts

Nitza Zakein's Haroset from Kurdistan

Nitza makes this haroset the way her husband's family did, in *Zakho*, in *Kurdistan*.

> *Silan* (bought date syrup)
> Roasted pistachios (or peanuts)
> Roasted walnuts
> Roasted black sesame

Grind the roasted nuts and black sesame, then add to the *silan*. Cook for an hour with a little water, taking care it does not stick to the bottom of the pan.

Shevi Ben Shmuel's Haroset from Persian Kurdistan

Shevi Ben Shmuel told me her family came from *Persian Kurdistan*. Their name had been Shmueli (which begins with a letter near the end of the Hebrew alphabet), but they changed it to Ben Shmuel (to begin with a letter at the beginning of the alphabet) at the time of the ḥaluka[1] so that they would be at the top, instead of the bottom, of the list for distribution of money. Hers was the only haroset to use fresh dates.

> Fresh dates
> Walnuts
> Cinnamon
> Wine (added in the kitchen)

HAROSET FROM PERSIA

Esther Cohen's Pomegranate Haroset from Shiraz

Esther Cohen from *Shiraz* in *Persia* gave me this family recipe for haroset, together with her secret, which she said she had not told anyone else. Esther saves pomegranates from the autumn festival of Sukkot. Her secret is that she peels them at Sukkot when they are fresh and not dried up, so it is much easier to do this, and then saves them in special new jars in the freezer until Passover. (The Ashkenazic Tosafists were the first to mention using pomegranates in haroset.)

> Apples
> Pears
> Cinnamon
> Peeled almonds (unroasted)
> Black raisins
> Pomegranates

---

1. *Ḥaluka* (distribution) referred to the money collected in Jewish Diaspora communities since at least the seventeenth century for distribution to scholars and the poor in the Land of Israel.

Blend all the ingredients except the pomegranates. Add the pomegranates, either with their seeds, or sieved to get rid of them, depending on the tastes of the people present.

Yaakov Dayan's Pomegranate Haroset from Teheran

Yaakov Dayan from *Teheran, Persia,* used to make this haroset for his family. After his death, his widow Tamar gave me his recipe as far as she remembered it. The nuts were originally ground with pestle and mortar. Tamar said that some people still do this, but Yaakov put them through the meat mincer.

> Walnuts
> Peanuts
> Pistachios
> Raisins
> Pomegranates
> Ginger
> Sweet red wine

Wash and dry nuts (unroasted) and grind them. Add washed and dried raisins with pomegranates from the last summer. Add ginger, pounded with pestle and mortar, or the bought powder. Mix until the consistency is like dough. Everyone adds as much red wine as he or she wants to his or her own plate at table.

Esther Berukhim's Haroset, Called *Ilḥo,* from Kerman

Esther Berukhim is from the Shimoni family who came from *Kerman* in *Persia.* She told me their haroset was called *ilḥo,* but gave me no details of how it was made, only how it was sourced. On the festival of Simḥat Torah, the Rejoicing of the Law, the men dance round the synagogue with the Torah scrolls. When they have finished dancing, they put the most beautiful apples and pomegranates on top of the Torah scrolls in their ornamented boxes. These are saved, and used for haroset on Passover six months later. When people made their haroset with a pestle and mortar, she said, the men and women used to make it together. Then came hand meat grinders and then electric blenders. The women no longer need help and do it all themselves.

> Apples
> Pomegranates

HAROSET FROM SYRIA

Miriam Mizrahi's Sephardic Haroset
Miriam Mizrahi came from *Haleb* (Aleppo) in *Syria*. Her daughter Aviva told me how she made her haroset.

> Dates
> Walnuts
> Cinnamon

Cook the dates in water, strain them and serve with walnuts and cinnamon sprinkled on top "for decoration."

HAROSET FROM IRAQ

Eveline Tufiq's Sephardic Haroset
The daughter of Eveline Tufiq from *Baghdad* in *Iraq* told me what her mother had told her about making haroset. A man used to go round the Jewish community selling dates, which he would tread for them to a mass between palm leaves. This was strained, and crushed nuts were added. (Maimonides also talks about treading dates for haroset.)

> Dates
> Nuts

HAROSET FROM THE IRAQI DIASPORA

Devora-Zippora Nehemiah's Two Recipes for Haroset from Cochin
Devora-Zippora Nehemiah's family lived for generations in *Ernaculum* in *Cochin* in *India* in a community that originated in Iraq. Her daughter

Rivka told me how she made her two sorts of haroset. She told me that squeezing the date juice through the muslin and twisting the cloth was very hard work, and the men would help. The juice which came out was cooked all day, on and off the heat. They did not add anything else, such as wine, apples, etc.

Recipe 1

Two packets of dried dates

Soak dates for half an hour in a stainless steel pan one quarter full of water. Break up the dates and squeeze through a muslin cloth. Cook the juice that comes out for a long time until thick. It is done when it does not come off on the fingers when touched.

Recipe 2: Haroset called valeichi
This form of haroset called *valeichi* was less common than the first sort.

Date juice haroset as in recipe 1 above
Almonds
Cashews
Sesame
Peanuts

Fry all the nuts until brown, crush them, then add to the date juice haroset above. This is much thicker.

HAROSET FROM ISRAEL
Yael Entebbe née Ben Tzion's family have lived in *Jerusalem* for eleven generations; her husband's family have lived there for thirteen generations. I met their daughter Adi on Purim, at a women's reading of the Megilla (Book of Esther), which she read in an unusual tune. She told me she came from an old Sephardic family. She did not know how her mother makes her haroset, but immediately got hold of her on her mobile phone to find out.

Yael Entebbe's Sephardic Haroset from Jerusalem

Date paste
Wine
Matza meal
Nuts

Mix the (bought) date paste with wine. Add matza meal and any nuts.

HAROSET FROM EGYPT

Claudia Roden's Sephardic Haroset from Alexandria

Claudia Roden from *Alexandria* in *Egypt,* on the Nile Delta, told me that her family's haroset had to be the reddish-brown color of the mud of the River Nile. As a professional food historian and chef, she gives an exact recipe in her book, *The Book of Jewish Food.*[2]

250 g (9 oz) pitted dates, chopped
250 g (9 oz) large yellow raisins or sultanas
125 ml (4 fl oz) sweet red Passover wine
60 g (2 oz) walnuts, coarsely chopped

Put the dates and sultanas with the wine in a pan. Add just a little water to cover. Cook on a very low heat, stirring occasionally, until the dates fall apart into a mush. Cook until it thickens to a soft paste. Pour into a bowl and sprinkle with the walnuts.

Ruhama Hayoun's Sephardic Haroset from Cairo

Ruhama's daughter, Michal Baranes, gave me her mother's recipe. Michal was younger than some of my other informants, and she had the instructions written down with exact quantities for almost all the ingredients. When she gave me the recipe, she added: "We eat it all Passover."

---

2. Claudia Roden, *The Book of Jewish Food: An Odyssey from Samarkand and Vilna to the Present Day* (London: Viking, 1997), 532.

200 gm black seedless raisins
½ kilo dates
1½ cups sugar
1 cup sweet red wine
Roughly crushed walnuts

Soak raisins overnight. Grind with dates and add sugar. Cook this with the water from the raisins until it is of the consistency of jam. Add walnuts.

HAROSET FROM LIBYA

Kamuna Vaturi's Sephardic Haroset from Tripoli

Kamuna Vaturi came from a family of kabbalist rabbis from *Tripoli* in *Libya*. Her daughter Dina Lavi told me she made her haroset with a pestle and mortar, just as they did in the Middle Ages, because it doesn't taste the same when made with machines. She then adds *bahar* (allspice) bought as a powder from a Tripolitan grocer, but not too much, as it is very strong. If it is not available, she uses cinnamon.

Dates
Almonds
Walnuts
Raisins
A little apple
A little *bahar* (allspice) or cinnamon

Pound dates, almonds, walnuts and raisins with a little apple. Add *bahar* (allspice). Combine with a wooden spoon and form into balls slightly smaller than a ping-pong ball, with hands oiled with olive oil. Thin down the balls with sweet wine at the table.

Nitza Zakein's Sephardic Haroset from Libya

We already met Nitza Zakein giving us her husband's recipe for haroset from Kurdistan. Nitza herself comes from *Benghazi* in *Libya*, where they made a quite different haroset, kneading it "like you knead pastry." (Maimonides also talked of kneading the haroset with wine or vinegar.)

Dates
Nuts
Sweet red wine
Cloves

Wash dates, then knead them with nuts and sweet red wine. Add cloves and make into balls, one for each person at the Seder.

HAROSET FROM TUNISIA

Linette (née Cohen)'s Sephardic Haroset from Jerba

Linette née Cohen is from *Jerba* in *Tunisia*. Jerba is an island where there is community of Jews who are all priests (*kohanim*). "I used to be a *kohenet* (female *kohen*)," she said, "but I gave it up when I married a man who was not a priest."

Linette makes her haroset of the consistency of chocolate spread, without oil, as it is already very heavy. She adds her own spices, but told me that you can now buy ready-made "spice for haroset" sold in the shop by weight. She only adds sesame to half the quantity because not all the children like it. She kneads her haroset and serves it as balls (just as we saw in some medieval Haggadas in chapter 2).

Dates
Almonds
Pistachios
Walnuts
Raisins
Grape juice or sweet red wine
Ground cloves
A little Yemenite *hawaij* (ground ginger, cardamom and cinnamon)

Optional:
Oil
Sesame

Grind dates, nuts and raisins finely with meat grinder. Add grape juice or sweet wine and oil if desired. Add a small amount of spices, and sesame if desired. Knead, and serve as balls.

HAROSET FROM ALGERIA

Eli Zanou's Bnei Tzion Haroset from Tafilalet

Eli (Jean-Louis) Zanou, from *Tafilalet* in *Algeria*, told me that in Algeria there were two major Sephardic communities, the Bnei Tzion and the Bnei Rahamim. Eli himself belonged to the Bnei Tzion who always went by the rulings of the Hida (whom we met in chapter 4). While eating the haroset, it was customary to throw the bitter herbs out of the window. You could tell from the position of the lettuce leaves on the pavement the next morning whether the Jews in the building lived on the first, second or third floor, Eli said. Throwing things was considered to bring good luck, he said, like the High Priest throwing blood in the Temple on the Day of Atonement (Yom Kippur). Eli was the only person I met to mention blood in the context of his haroset, and even here, this was not a direct connection.

The Bnei Rahamim, Eli added, used plums or prunes, while a small community of Jews living in Zab were reputed to put grit in their haroset. (Rabbi Menahem MiLonzano and the Hida were against putting grit into haroset.)

> Dates
> Figs
> Nuts
> Wine

Add wine at table, as this is otherwise very dry.

HAROSET FROM MOROCCO

Alya Kazula's Sephardic Haroset

Alya Kazula née Levi, whose family came from *Morocco*, and who is married to an Algerian, told me they used to have Algerian haroset while her mother-in-law was still alive, but now they make the Moroccan version. Whoever is available makes it: she, her husband, or her daughter. During the Seder, they thin it down with sweet red wine at the table. (This is exactly the procedure recommended by the Tosafists, to harmonize the conflict of opinion in the Jerusalem Talmud that haroset should be both thick and fluid – it was made thick, then thinned down at table.)

> Dates
> Walnuts
> Ginger
> A little cinnamon
> Sweet red wine

Grind dates, walnuts, ginger and a little cinnamon, and form into balls.

HAROSET FROM YEMEN

The Rada Family's Sephardic Haroset

The Rada family from *Yemen*, who live in the Yemenite community in Rosh HaAyin, make their haroset together, as they have always done.

(We remember Rabbi Yosef Kappah, the Yemenite rabbi who interpreted the Jerusalem Talmud's discussion on haroset in chapter 1 to read: "She grinds it with him.")

> Dates
> Ginger
> Wine

Hamama Madari's Haroset, Called
Dukkeh, from Alina in the Yemen

Hamama Madari's daughter Naomi Gozi told me how her mother (from the village of *Alina* in *Yemen*) prepared her haroset, which she calls *dukkeh* (as in the Jerusalem Talmud). Naomi used to prepare it just as her mother did; now her husband makes it to help her. In Yemen, wrote Naomi, the women cooked and prepared everything by themselves.

> Almonds
> Raisins
> Dates
> Walnuts

Ginger
Karsa (cinnamon)

Grind each ingredient separately, then mix into a single mixture. Add red wine slowly until it looks like clay, then add spices like straw in memory of the straw they used in Egypt.

HAROSET FROM NEW ZEALAND

Estelle Asher's Ashkenazic Haroset with Spanish Ancestry

Estelle Asher comes from the *Montanjees* family, named after a small town in *Spain*. They moved to *Amsterdam*, then *England*, where her father Benjamin Montanjees married Vera Perlman, of *Polish* origin, in Bevis Marks Synagogue, before immigrating to *New Zealand*, as we saw in chapter 5. Her Sephardic hazelnuts survived the long journey through the Diaspora.

Apples
Red wine
Cinnamon
Hazelnuts

HAROSET FROM GERMANY

Aharon Oppenheimer's Untasted *Yekkish* (German Jewish) Haroset

Ingredients: unknown

Aharon Oppenheimer, whose family came from *Berlin, Germany*, told me that he did not know what his mother put in her haroset. "No doubt," he said, "it was delicious, but we never ate it. We merely dipped the bitter herbs in it and shook it off." This custom is mentioned in various Haggadas, and Ruti Rosenblatt née Munk, whose family came from *Frankfurt*, confirmed that other *Yekkes* (German Jews) took this instruction literally and did not eat their haroset: "Otherwise it would take away the bitterness of the bitter herbs," she said. (Rav Pappa in the Babylonian Talmud said you should not leave the bitter herbs too long in the haroset, just in case the sweetness of the spice destroys the bitterness of the herbs.)

Bibliography

Amar, Z. "Ibn al-Baytar and the Study of the Plants of Al-Sham." *Cathedra* 76 (1985): 49–76.

An Australian Aristologist. *Hebrew Cookery*. London/Melbourne: Low & Co./George Robertson, 1867.

Archestratus *Fragments from the Life of Luxury*. Edited by J. Wilkins and S. Hill. Totnes: Prospect Books, 2011.

Athenaeus. *The Deipnosophists*. Translated by C. B. Gulick. London/New York: Heinemann/G. P. Putnam, 1928.

Avital, M. *Passover Haggada of Kupat Ḥolim* (*Haggada shel Pesaḥ shel Kupat Ḥolim*). Merkaz Kupat Ḥolim: no place, no date, no page numbers. Acquired by Tel Aviv University Library in 1971.

Azulai, Hayim Joseph David ben Isaac. *The Lap* (lit. *Knees*) *of Joseph* (*Sefer Birkei Yosef*). Livorno: G. V. Falorni, 1774. Repr. Jerusalem: Makhon Ḥatam Sofer, 1969.

Azulai, Hayim Joseph David ben Isaac. *The Joy of the Pilgrim Festival* (*Simḥat HaRegel*). Livorno: A. I. Castillio and A. Saadon, 1781.

Benedict, B. Z. "Introduction to the Collectors' Book (*Sefer Baalei HaAsufot*)." *Sinai* 27 (1950): 322–9.

Benjamin of Tudela *The Itinerary*. Translated and edited by M. N. Adler. London: H. Frowde, 1907. Repr. New York: Feldheim, 1964.

Ben Shalom, R. "The Ritual Murder Accusation at Arles and the Franciscan Mission at Avignon in 1453: Paris MS. Héb. 631" ("Alilat

HaDam BeArl VeHaMisyon HaFrantziskani BeAvinyon BiShnat 1453"). *Zion* 63 (1996): 391–407.

Bohak, G. *Ancient Jewish Magic.* Cambridge: Cambridge University Press, 2008.

Bokser, B. *The Origins of the Seder: The Passover Rite and Early Rabbinic Judaism.* Berkeley: University of California Press, 1984.

G. Bos, M. Hussein, G. Mensching, and F. Savelsberg, ed. and com. *Medical Synonym Lists for Medieval Provence*: Shem Tov ben Isaac of Tortosa: *Sefer Ha-Shimmush* Book 29. Leiden: Brill, 2011.

Boyarin, D. "The Talmud as a Fat Rabbi: A Novel Approach." *Text & Talk* 5 (2008): 603–19.

Buccini, A. F. "The Bitter – and Flatulent – Aphrodisiac: Synchrony and Diachrony of the Culinary Use of *Muscari Comosum* in Greece and Italy." In *Vegetables: Proceeding of the Oxford Symposium on Food and Cookery 2008*, edited by S. R. Friedland, 46–55. Totnes: Prospect Books, 2009.

Cernea, R. Fredman. *The Passover Seder: An Anthropological Perspective on Jewish Culture.* Lanham: University Press of America, 1995. Originally published as R. Fredman Gruber, *The Passover Seder: Afikoman in Exile.* Philadelphia: University of Pennsyvania Press, 1981.

Cimok, F., ed. *Antioch Mosaics.* Istanbul: A Turizm Yayınları, 1995.

Cohen, R. I. "Urban Visibility and Biblical Visions: Jewish Culture in Western and Central Europe in the Modern Age." In *Cultures of the Jews: A New History*, edited by D. Biale, 731–96. New York: Schocken Books, 2002.

Columella. *De Re Rustica.* Translated by E. M. Forster and E. H. Heffner. London/Cambridge: Heinemann/Harvard University Press, 1955.

Cooper, J. *Eat and Be Satisfied: A Social History of Jewish Food.* New Jersey/London: Jason Aronson, 1973.

Dalby, A. *Food in the Ancient World from A to Z.* London: Routledge, 2003.

Dalby, A. *Dangerous Tastes: The Story of Spices.* London: The British Museum Press, 2000. Repr. 2002.

Dalby, A. *Siren Feasts: A History of Food and Gastronomy in Greece.* London/New York: Routledge, 1996. Repr. 1997.

David HaNagid. *Midrash on the Passover Haggada.* Translated from the Arabic into Hebrew by S. Barh"i Yerushalmi. Jerusalem: Wagshal, 1981.

Davidson, A. *The Oxford Companion to Food.* Oxford: Oxford University Press, 1999.

Dinur, B. Z. *Israel in the Diaspora (Yisrael BaGola).* Tel Aviv/Jerusalem: Dvir, 1966.

Elazar ben Judah. *The Book of the Apothecary (Sefer HaRoke'aḥ).* Edited by S. Schneursohn. Jerusalem: Otzar HaPoskim, 1967.

Eliezer ben Joel HaLevi. *Ravia's Book (Sefer Ravia).* Edited by A. Aptowitzer. Berlin: Mekitzei Nirdamim, 1938. Repr. Jerusalem: Makhon Harry Fischel, 1964.

Eliezer ben Nathan. *The Stone of Help: Ravan's Book (Even HaEzer: Sefer Ravan).* Prague: Moshe Katz, 1610. Repr. New York: Grossman, 1958.

Elijah of London. *The Writings.* Edited by M. Y. L. Sacks with C. Roth. Jerusalem: Mosad HaRav Kook, 1956.

Elijah ben Solomon Zalman of Vilna. *Commentaries on Aggadot (Biurei Aggadot).* Jerusalem: unknown publisher, 1971.

Elijah ben Solomon Zalman of Vilna. *Passover Haggada (Seder Haggada shel Pesaḥ).* Edited by N. Pfeffer. New York: Makhon HaGra, 1999.

Emanuel, S., ed. *The New Responsa of the Geonim (Teshuvot HaGeonim HaḤadashot): MS. Moscow 566.* Jerusalem: Makhon Ofek, 1995.

Epstein, M. M. *The Medieval Haggadah: Art, Narrative and Religious Imagination.* New Haven/London: Yale University Press, 2011.

Esposito, M. "Un Process Contre les Juifs de la Savoie en 1329." *Revue d'Histoire Écclesiastique* 34 (1938): 785–95.

Fairley, B. "Heine and the Festive Board," *University of Toronto Quarterly,* 36 (1967): 209–19.

Feliks, Y., ed. *Jerusalem Talmud: Tractate Shevi'it (Talmud Yerushalmi: Masekhet Shevi'it).* Jerusalem: Rubin Mass, 1986).

Feliks, Y. *Spice, Forest and Garden Trees: Plants in Biblical and Rabbinic Literature (Atzei Besamim, Yaar VeNoi: Tzimḥei HaTanakh VeḤazal).* Jerusalem: Rubin Mass, 1997.

Fireside, B. J., and S. Costello *Private Joel and the Sewell Mountain Seder*. Minneapolis: Kar-Ben Publishing, 2008.

Freedman, P. *Out of the East: Spices and the Medieval Imagination*. New Haven/London: Yale University Press, 2008.

Friedland, S. R., ed. *Vegetables: Proceeding of the Oxford Symposium on Food and Cookery 2008*. Totnes: Prospect Books, 2009.

Friedman, S. *Ancient Tosefta* (Tosefta Atikta). Ramat Gan: Bar Ilan University Press, 2002.

Gaster, M. *Studies and Texts in Folklore, Magic, Medieval Romance, Hebrew Apocrypha and Samaritan Archaeology*, vol. 3. London: Maggs Bros, 1928. Repr. New York: Ktav, 1971: 221; 226–7.

Goldin, F. "My Father's *Kharoset*." *Jewish Quarterly* 205 (2007): 88.

Goldschmidt, E. D., ed. *Passover Haggada: Its Sources and History* (*Haggada shel Pesaḥ: Mekoroteha VeToldoteha*). Jerusalem: Mosad Bialik, 1969.

Goldschmidt, E. D., ed. *Seder Rav Amram Gaon*. Jerusalem: Mosad HaRav Kook, 1971.

Golinkin, D. "Pesah Potpourri: On the Origin and Development of Some Lesser-Known Pesah Customs." *Conservative Judaism* 55/3 (2003): 58–71.

Goodman, P., ed. *The Passover Anthology*. Philadelphia: Jewish Publication Society of America, 1973.

Grocock, C., and S. Grainger, trans. and eds. *Apicius: A Critical Edition with Introduction and English Translations*. Totnes: Prospect Books, 2006.

Harrison, S. G., G. B. Masefield and M. Wallis. *The Oxford Book of Food Plants*. London: Peerage Books, 1985.

Hazan, Jacob ben Judah MiLondres. *Etz Ḥayim*. Edited by I. Brodie. Jerusalem: Mosad HaRav Kook, 1962–67.

Heine, H. *Werke: In fünfzehn Teilen*. Berlin: Deutsches Verlaghaus Bong, 1908.

Heller, Yom Tov Lipman ben Nathan HaLevi. *Tosefot Yom Tov*. See Ovadiah ben Abraham Yareh MiBertinoro and Yom Tov Lipman Heller.

Huffington Post. https://www.huffingtonpost.com/2015/04/01/charoset-ben-and-jerrys-is-the-real-deal_n_6977854.html (accessed April 2018).

Isaac ben Moses. *The Light Is Sown* (*Or Zarua*). Edited by A. Marienberg. Jerusalem: Yeshivat Or Etzion, 2006.

Isaac, B., and Y. Shahar, eds. *Judaea-Palaestina, Babylon and Rome: Jews in Antiquity*. Tübingen, 2012.

Isserlein, Israel ben Petahya, see Joseph ben Moses, *The Collection of Righteousness* (*Sefer Leket Yosher*).

Jachter, H. https://www.koltorah.org/halachah/the-mitzvah-of-charoset-by-rabbi-chaim-jachter (accessed April 2018).

Jewish Encyclopedia Online. http://www.jewishencyclopedia.com/articles/6571-gematria (accessed April 2018).

Joseph ben David. *Beit David*. Salonica: Betzalel Ashkenazi Press, 1740.

Joseph ben Moses. *The Collection of Righteousness* (*Sefer Leket Yosher*), "Including the *Minhagim*, Halakhic Rulings and Responsa of the *Gaon*, his Rabbi [Israel ben Petahya Isserlein], Author of *Terumot HaDeshen* [Sweeping the Ashes]." Edited by J. Freimann. Berlin: Itzkowski, 1903. Repr. Jerusalem: no publisher, 1964.

Kalonymos ben Kalonymos. *The Touchstone* (*Even Bohan*). Edited by A. M. Habermann. Tel Aviv: Maḥberot LaSifrut, 1956.

Kappah, Y., ed. *Mishna with Maimonides' Commentary* (*Mishna im Perush Rabbenu Moshe ben Maimon*). Jerusalem: Mosad HaRav Kook, 1963.

Kappah, Y. *Passover Haggada* (*Sefer Aggadeta DePisḥa*). Jerusalem: HaAguda LeHatzalat Ginzei Teiman, 1958.

Kirshenblatt-Gimblett, B. "Hebrew Cookery: An Early Jewish Cookbook from the Antipodes." *Petits Propos Culinaires* 28 (1988): 11–21.

Kogman-Appel, K. *Die zweite Nürnberger und die Jehuda Haggada: Jüdische Illustratoren zwischen Tradition und Fortschritt*. Frankfurt am Main: P. Lang, 1998.

Kogman-Appel, K. *Illuminated Haggadot from Medieval Spain: Biblical Imagery and the Passover Holiday*. Pennsylvania: Pennsylvania University Press, 2006.

de Lange, N. *Greek Jewish Texts from the Cairo Genizah*. Tübingen: Mohr Siebeck, 1996.

Laski, M. "Seder at Grandpa's." In *The Passover Anthology*, edited by P. Goodman. Philadelphia: Jewish Publication Society of America, 1973.

Laurioux, B. "Spices in the Medieval Diet: A New Approach." *Food and Foodways* 1 (1985): 43–76.

Laurioux, B. "Cuisines médiévales." In *Histoire de l'Alimentation*, edited by J. L. Flandrin and M. Montanari, 459–77. Paris: Fayard, 1996.

Levin, I., ed. *Blood and Fire and Columns of Smoke: The Passover Holocaust Haggada* (*Dam VaEsh VeTimrot Ashan: Haggadat HaShoah LaPesaḥ*). Tel Aviv: Yediot Aḥaronot, 2008.

Lieberman, S. *HaYerushalmi Kifshuto*, vol. I. Jerusalem: Darom, 2008, 3rd edition.

Lowenstein, S. M. *The Jewish Cultural Tapestry: International Jewish Folk Traditions.* Oxford/New York: Oxford University Press, 2000.

Maimonides, M. *Commentary on the Mishna* (*Perush al HaMishna*). Edited by D. Biton and E. Kerah. Jerusalem: Makhon Maor, 2009.

Maimonides, M. *Mishneh Torah.* Edited by M. D. Rabinowitz and ten other editors. Jerusalem: Mosad HaRav Kook, 1957.

Makhon HaEntziklopedya HaTalmudit. *Talmudic Encyclopedia* (*Entziklopedya Talmudit*), vol. 8. Edited by S. J. Zevin. Jerusalem: Yad HaRav Hertzog, 1957.

Mamet, D. *Passover.* New York: St Martin's Press, 1995.

Mamet, D. *Three Uses of the Knife: On the Nature and Purpose of Drama.* New York: Vintage Books, 2000.

Manoah ben Simeon Badrashi. *The Book of Rest* (*Sefer HaMenuḥa*) =Collection of Rishonim on Mishneh Torah 1 (*Kovetz Rishonim al Mishneh Torah*). Jerusalem: unknown publisher, 1967.

Margaritha, A. *Der Ganz Jüdisch Glaub.* Augspurg: unknown publisher, 1530.

Meldula, J., de Amsterdam, ed. and trans. *Orden de la Agada de Pesah, en Hebraico y Español, segun uzan los Judios, Españoles, y Portuguezes, traducido del Hebraico y Caldeo.* London: L. Alexander, 1813.

Meiseles, I. *The Poetry of Rabbi Elazar ben Judah of Worms* (*Shirat HaRoke'aḥ*). Jerusalem: unknown publisher, 1993.

Ménagier de Paris. translation at http://www.daviddfriedman.com/ Medieval/Cookbooks/Menagier/Menagier.html (accessed April 2018).

Metzger, M. *La Haggada enluminée.* Leiden: Brill, 1973.

Metzger, T., and M. Metzger. *Jewish Life in the Middle Ages: Illuminated Hebrew Manuscripts of the Thirteenth to the Sixteenth Centuries.* New Jersey: Fine Art Books, 1982.

Meyerhof, M., ed., trans. and com. *Sarh Asma al-Uqqar (l'Explication des Noms de Drogues): Un Glossaire de Matière Médicale Composé par Maïmonide: Mémoires Présentés à l'Institut d'Égypte 41.* Cairo: Imprimerie de l'Institut Française d'Archéologie Orientale, 1940.

Milton, G. *Nathaniel's Nutmeg: How One Man's Courage Changed the Course of History.* London: Hodder and Stoughton, 1999.

Molin, Jacob. *The Maharil's Book: Customs (Sefer Maharil: Minhagim).* Edited by S. Spitzer. Jerusalem: Makhon Yerushalayim, 1989.

Montefiore, J. Cohen. *The Jewish Manual or Practical Information in Jewish and Modern Cookery, with a Collection of Valuable Recipes and Hints Relating to the Toilette.* Edited by a Lady. London: T. & W. Boone, 1846. Repr. no place: Bibliobazaar, 2006.

Munro, J. "Oriental Spices and Their Costs in Medieval Cuisine: Luxuries or Necessities?" Lecture given at the University of Toronto, 1988, posted at https://www.economics.utoronto.ca/munro5/ SPICES1.htm (accessed April 2018).

Nachama, A., J. H. Schoeps, H. Simon, eds. *Jews in Berlin.* Berlin: Henschel, 2002.

Nasrallah, N. *Annals of the Caliphs' Kitchens: Ibn Sayyar al-Warraq's Tenth-Century Baghdadi Cookbook.* Leiden/Boston: Brill, 2010.

Nasrallah, N. *Treasure Trove of Benefits and Variety at the Table: A Fourteenth-Century Egyptian Cookbook.* Leiden/Boston: Brill, 2018.

Nathan, J. *Quiches, Kugel and Couscous: My Search for Jewish Cooking in France.* New York: Knopf, 2010.

NewYorkTimes.com http://www.nytimes.com/2011/04/09/nyregion/ 09haggadah.html?_r=3&hp& (accessed April, 2018).

Onthemainline blog: http://onthemainline.blogspot.co.il/2013/02/pesach-is-in-air-so-civil-war-seder-1862.html (accessed April 2018).

Ophir, A. "From Pharaoh to Saddam Hussein: The Reproduction of the Other in the Passover Haggadah." In *The Other in Jewish Thought and History: Constructions of Jewish Culture and Identity*, edited by L. J. Silberstein and R. L. Cohn: 205–35. New York: New York University Press, 1994.

Ovadiah ben Abraham Yareh MiBertinoro and Yom Tov Lipman Heller. *Commentary on the Mishna (Perush al HaMishna)*. Edited by Y. Feliks. Jerusalem: Midrash Benei Tzion, 1967.

Paston-Williams, S. *The Art of Dining: A History of Cooking and Eating*. London: National Trust, 1995.

Penkower, J. S. "A Note Regarding R. Menahem de Lonzano." http://seforim.blogspot.co.il/2009/08/jordan-s-penkower-note-regarding-r.html (accessed April 2018).

Pliny. *Natural History*. Translated by W. H. S. Jones. Cambridge/London: Harvard University Press/Heinemann, 1969).

de Pomis, D. *The Shoot of David (Tzemaḥ David): Dittionario Novo Hebraico*. Venice: Ioannes de Gara, 1587.

Proust, M. *Remembrance of Things Past: Swann's Way (=À la recherche du temps perdu: du côté de chez Swann)*. Translated by C. K. Scott-Moncrieff. New York: Random House, 1934.

Rabbinowicz, R. N. N. *Dikdukei Soferim*. München: A. Huber, K. Hof Buchdrucker, 1874.

Riley, G., ed. *The Oxford Companion to Italian Food*. New York: Oxford University Press, 2007.

Roden, C. *A New Book of Middle Eastern Food*. Harmondsworth: Penguin, 1985.

Roden, C. *The Book of Jewish Food: An Odyssey from Samarkand and Vilna to the Present Day*. London: Viking, 1997.

Rodinson, M., A. J. Arberry and C. Perry. *Medieval Arab Cookery*. Totnes: Prospect Books, 2001.

Roth, C., ed. *The Sarajevo Haggadah*. Beograd: Izdavacki Zavod, 1963.

Saadia Gaon. *Rabbi Saadia Gaon's Prayerbook* (*Siddur Rav Saadia Gaon*). Edited by I. Davidson, S. Assaf and B. I. Joel. Jerusalem: ḥevrat Mekitzei Nirdamim, 1941.

Schäfer, G., and S. Weingarten. "Celebrating Purim and Passover: Food and Memory in the Creation of Jewish Identity." In *Celebration: Proceedings of the Oxford Symposium on Food and Cookery 2011*, edited by M. McWilliams, 316–25. Totnes: Prospect Books, 2012.

Schaffer, A. "The History of Horseradish as the Bitter Herb of Passover." *Gesher* 8 (1981): 217–37.

Schorsch, I. *From Text to Context: The Turn to History in Modern Judaism*. Hanover: Brandeis University Press, 1994.

Schwartz, S. *Imperialism and Jewish Society 200 BCE–640 CE: Jews, Christians and Muslims from the Ancient to the Modern World*. Princeton: Princeton University Press, 2001.

Scully, T. *The Art of Cookery in the Middle Ages*. Woodbridge: Boydell Press, 1995. Repr. 2002.

Simeon ben Tzemah Duran. *The Book About Leaven* (*Sefer Maamar Ḥametz*). Livorno: unknown publisher, 1744. Repr. Jerusalem: Makhon Ḥatam Sofer, 1969.

Smith, D. *From Symposium to Eucharist: The Banquet in the Early Christian World*. Minneapolis: Fortress Press, 2002.

Sokoloff, M. *Dictionary of Jewish Babylonian Aramaic in the Talmudic and Geonic Periods*. Ramat Gan: Bar Ilan University Press, 2002.

Soloveitchik, H. *Principles and Pressures: Jewish Trade in Gentile Wine in the Middle Ages* (*Yeinam: Saḥar BeYeinam shel Goyim: Al Gilgulah shel Halakha BeOlam HaMaaseh*). Tel Aviv: Am Oved, 2003.

Soloveitchik, J. *Nefesh HaRav*. Edited by T. Shechter. Jerusalem, Reishit Yerushalayim, 1993.

Stein, S. "The Influence of Symposia Literature on the Literary Form of the Pesah Haggadah." *Journal of Jewish Studies* 8 (1957): 13–44.

Stemberger, G. *Introduction to the Talmud and the Midrash*. Edinburgh: T. & T. Clark, 1996.

Sternhartz, N. *Passover Haggada: The Light Shines* (*Seder Haggada shel Pesaḥ: Or Zore'aḥ*), with comments and explanations of Rabbi Nahman of Breslov. Jerusalem: unknown publisher, 1926.

Strauss, H. "Passover in the Ghettoes of the 'General Government'" ("Hag HaPesah BeGetaot HaGeneral Guvernmant"). *Massuah Annual* 8 (1980): 83–102.

Sutton, D. E. *Remembrance of Repasts: An Anthropology of Food and Memory.* Oxford/New York: Berg, 2001.

Tabory, J. "Towards a History of the Paschal Meal." In *Passover and Easter: Origin and History to Modern Times,* edited by P. F. Bradshaw and L. Hoffman, 62–80. Notre Dame: University of Notre Dame Press, 1999.

Tabory, J. *JPS Commentary on the Haggadah: Historical Introduction, Translation and Commentary.* Philadelphia: Jewish Publication Society, 2008.

Tamir, M. "Memories of the Sounds, Sights and Smells of Passover." *Kibbutz Afikim Passover Leaflet.* Kibbutz Afikim: self-published, 1997.

Teitelbaum, H. *Responsa Yad Hanokh.* Edited by A. M. Meisels. Brooklyn: unknown publisher, 2000.

Trachtenberg, J. *Jewish Magic and Superstition: A Study in Folk Religion.* New York: Behrman's Jewish Book House, 1939.

Valençin, D., ed. *Orden dela Hagadah de noche de Pascoa de Pesah. Tradusida dela original Hebraica conforme la ordenaron nuestros Sabios.* Livorno: Gio. Vincenza Bonfigli, 1654.

Viandier de Taillevent. Bibliothèque Nationale MS. Translated by J. Prescott. http://www.telusplanet.net/public/prescotj/data/viandier/viandier5.html (accessed April 2018).

Visotzky, B. L. "Most Tender and Fairest of Women: A Study in the Transmission of Aggada." *Harvard Theological Review* 76 (1983): 403–18.

Vital, Hayim. *The Book of the Fruit of the Tree of Life (Sefer Peri Etz Hayim).* From the version on the CD-ROM of HaTaklitor HaTorani. Jerusalem: D. B. S. Mahshevim, no date.

Weilerstein, S. R. *What the Moon Brought.* Philadelphia: Jewish Publication Society of America, 1942.

Weingarten, M. Y. *The Arranged Seder (HaSeder HeArukh).* Jerusalem: M. Y. Weingarten, 1993.

Weingarten, S. "'In Thy Blood, Live!' Haroset and the Blood Libels." *Revue des Études Juives* 172, 1–2 (2013): 83–100.

Weiss, A. *Women at Prayer: A Halakhic Analysis of Women's Prayer Groups.* Hoboken, NJ: Ktav, 1990.

Xenophon. *Cyropaedeia.* Translated by W. Miller. London: Heinemann, 1983.

Yerushalmi, Y. H. *Haggadah and History: A Panorama in Facsimile of Five Centuries of the Printed Haggadah from the Collections of Harvard University and the Jewish Theological Seminary of America.* Philadelphia: Jewish Publication Society of America, 1976.

Yuval, I. J. "Passover in the Middle Ages." In *Passover and Easter: Origin and History to Modern Times,* edited by P. F. Bradshaw and L. A. Hoffman, 127–60. Notre Dame: Notre Dame University Press, 1999.

Yuval, I. J. *Two Nations in Your Womb: Perceptions of Jews and Christians in the Middle Ages.* Berkeley: University of California Press, 2006.

Zanolini, A. *Lexicon Chaldaico-Rabbinicum.* Padua: Typis Seminarii, 1747.

Zedekiah ben Abraham Anav. *The Gleaned Ears (Shibbolei HaLeket).* Edited by S. Buber. Vilna: Widow and Brothers Rom, 1886. Repr. Jerusalem: Pe'er HaTorah, 1962.

Zohary, D., and M. Hopf. *Domestication of Plants in the Old World.* Oxford: Oxford University Press, 2000, 3rd edition.

Zondel, H., and A. L. Gordon. *Treasury of Prayers (Siddur Otzar HaTefillot).* Vilna: unknown publisher, 1910. Repr. Tel Aviv/Jerusalem: unknown publisher, 1960.

Zylberberg, S. "Oranges and Seders: Symbols of Jewish Women's Wrestlings." *Nashim* 5 (2002): 148–71.

Index

The fonts used in this book are from the Arno family